Elite • 168

World War II Street-Fighting Tactics

Stephen Bull · Illustrated by Peter Dennis

Consultant editor Martin Windrow

First published in Great Britain in 2008 by Osprey Publishing,
Midland House, West Way, Botley, Oxford OX2 0PH, UK
443 Park Avenue South, New York, NY 10016, USA
E-mail: info@ospreypublishing.com

A CIP catalogue record for this book is available from the British Library

ISBN: 978 1 84603 291 2

Editor: Martin Windrow
Page layout by Ken Vail Graphic Design, Cambridge, UK
Typeset in Helvetica Neue and ITC New Baskerville
Index by Glyn Sutcliffe
Originated by PPS Grasmere, Leeds, UK
Printed in China through World Print Ltd.

08 09 10 11 12   10 9 8 7 6 5 4 3 2 1

FOR A CATALOGUE OF ALL BOOKS PUBLISHED BY OSPREY MILITARY AND
AVIATION PLEASE CONTACT:

NORTH AMERICA
Osprey Direct, c/o Random House Distribution Center, 400 Hahn Road,
Westminster, MD 21157
E-mail: info@ospreydirect.com

ALL OTHER REGIONS
Osprey Direct UK, P.O. Box 140 Wellingborough, Northants, NN8 2FA, UK
E-mail: info@ospreydirect.co.uk

Osprey Publishing is supporting the Woodland Trust, the UK's leading
woodland conservation charity, by funding the dedication of trees.

www.ospreypublishing.com

Artist's note

Readers may care to note that the original paintings from
which the colour plates in this book were prepared are
available for private sale. All reproduction copyright
whatsoever is retained by the Publishers. All enquiries
should be addressed to:

Peter Dennis,
Fieldhead,
The Park,
Mansfield,
Notts
NG18 2AT,
UK

The Publishers regret that they can enter into no
correspondence upon this matter.

WORLD WAR II STREET-FIGHTING TACTICS

INTRODUCTION

'Street fighting' – known today by the acronyms FIBUA (Fighting in Built Up Areas) or MOUT (Military Operations in Urban Terrain) – has occurred since biblical times, and one of the first writers to refer to the subject in a tactical context was the Roman author Vegetius. The medieval, early modern and Napoleonic eras offer numerous examples of bloody fighting and appalling massacres in the streets of contested towns. During the 19th century, however, it was the engineering branches of armies that occupied a specialized niche not only in the prosecution of sieges, but in the attack and defence of ordinary civilian buildings. In 1853 a British officer, LtCol Jebb, RE, writing in the *Aide Memoire to the Military Sciences*, attempted to formulate universal and scientific principles for the conduct of the defence of buildings and villages.

Jebb's key maxims were: that forces should not be 'shut up' in built-up areas without a particular object; that the means of reinforcement and retreat were as crucial as the actual defence; that buildings required very different treatments depending on their relationship with an overall plan; and that the selection and preparation of any particular structures for defence was a 'great art', in which one might have to sacrifice almost anything to be successful. When it came to defending a building, Jebb saw little distinction between a church, a factory or a country house – all could be made defensible if six factors were taken into account:

3

RIGHT **A bullet-pocked building in the central Várhegy district of Buda, 2007. More than 100,000 soldiers and civilians were killed in the battle for Budapest, which began with its encirclement in December 1944, and ended with its fall to the Red Army on 13 February 1945. The German defence centred on the Buda side of the Danube, where a labyrinth of tunnels ran under the ancient castle. About 80 per cent of Budapest's buildings were damaged in what came to be regarded as the final rehearsal for the battle of Berlin.**

BELOW **Plan for the defence of a house 'not exposed to artillery fire', from the British *Manual of Field Engineering* (1939). The copious use of barbed wire, loopholes, steel loophole plates and traverses is suggestive of lengthy preparation – and draws extensively upon devices developed for the trenches of World War I. The thick apron of 'close wire' prevented enemy troops getting close enough to place charges or put grenades through narrow openings.**

(1) The building should 'command all that surrounds it'.

(2) The structure should be 'substantial', and furnish the materials needed.

(3) Its size should be proportionate to the number of defenders.

(4) It should have walls and projections suitable for flanking – i.e. positions from which enfilade fire could be brought to bear on the attacker.

(5) The approach should be difficult for the attacker, while the defender should maintain a route for 'safe retreat'.

(6) The situation should be suitable to the 'object for which the detachment is to be posted'.

In 1862 the same journal printed a counterpart article in which Gen Sir John F. Burgoyne elaborated principles for 'street fighting' and the 'attack and defence of open towns', citing illustrations from both Napoleonic and more recent examples. Burgoyne's approach was brutally realistic; he recognized that when committed inside a built-up area, confronted by 'tumults and insurrection' and often unable to tell bystanders from foes, troops were liable to respect 'neither person nor property'. The only satisfactory way to prevent loss of control was therefore not to bring the soldiery into an enemy or rebellious town until they were 'fully authorized to act'. Where facing determined opposition, attackers would do well to deploy 'sappers' provided with 'an assortment of crowbars, sledge-hammers, short ladders, and above all, some bags of powder'. These could work their way along continuous terraces of buildings, breaking through walls, while the infantry – avoiding column formations – fought in 'small detachments well supported'. The infantry could similarly help the engineers by keeping up fire against windows, preventing defenders from shooting out.

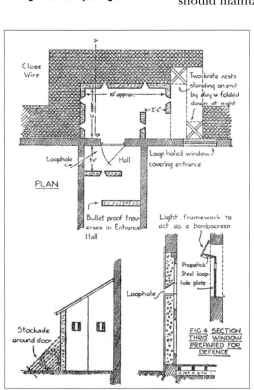

In some instances burning the whole town had much to recommend it. Many of Burgoyne's points would be demonstrated during May 1871, when the French Army of Versailles recaptured the streets of Paris from the rebellious Communards in 'Bloody Week'.

By World War I street fighting had a long and unedifying history, and it was natural that this particular form of combat should be increasingly codified and integrated into formal training. Grenades were standard issue for engineers long before 1914, while the modern flamethrower was perfected in the decade leading up to the war and unleashed in 1915. In Britain, Charles N. Watts published his *Notes on Street Fighting* in 1916. By this time British Army sniper training included lessons on built-up areas, and 'realistic environments' were specially created for practice. At the end of the Great War, US instructors took the idea a stage further with the introduction of the now-famous 'Hogan's Alley' concept. According to Maj J.S. Hatcher, this was originally the brainchild of a Capt Deming, 'an artist by profession', who had 'contributed much valuable material' to training by creating landscape targets. Back at Caldwell, New Jersey, in 1919, he constructed a 'French Village'. At the back of this was

> a pit for the scorers. Each of these scorers had a cardboard figure, resembling the head and shoulders of a man, nailed on the end of a long stick. The shooter took his place at the firing point, gun in hand. Suddenly at the windows or the corner of a wall, or some other unexpected place, one of these figures would be exposed for three seconds, then withdrawn… This is a very hard thing to do.

At Camp Perry, the US National Rifle Association would teach similar urban combat skills to police and civilian pistol shooters using this same 'Hogan's Alley' idea.

The last real opportunities to refine street-fighting techniques before 1939 came in the Spanish Civil War. Methods learned in, for instance, the defence of Madrid in 1936–37 would later be disseminated to British forces, both by veterans of the International Brigades working with the Home Guard, and subsequently through lectures at the Commando School. Subjects learned included demolition, barricades and urban sniping; but arguably the most important observations were made on the interactions of armour, aircraft and 'guerrilla' techniques in urban settings. In the opinion of Capt Tom Wintringham (the Great War veteran who had led the British 57th Bn in 15th International Bde until wounded at Jarama), in the face of new technologies the infantryman's best chance of survival was invisibility – and urban streets provided the best cover both from sight, and from the action of aircraft and tanks. Neither machine could carry enough munitions to destroy an entire town in one mission, and even if an area was flattened, the rubble and ruins could still be defended. Completely razing a city to the ground would take far more time than any modern mobile or 'blitz' army would be able to invest.

Some basic tips for the infantryman from Maj G.A. Wade's *House to House Fighting* (1940). Again, the drawings are only slight modifications of those produced during 1914–18 showing troops the correct way to treat traverses during the advance along a trench.

DO NOT LET YOUR BAYONET SHOW!

HOW TO APPROACH A CORNER.

HOW NOT TO LOOK ROUND

HOW TO LOOK ROUND.

'BLITZKRIEG' IN URBAN AREAS

German doctrine

The German 'lightning' campaigns of 1939–40 involved relatively little urban fighting. The siege of Warsaw and the defence of Calais were exceptional: this was no accident, as it was appreciated that street battles were costly, and could extend beyond a point to which forces prepared for short operations could properly be sustained. Nevertheless, a German doctrine for fighting in built-up areas, or *Ortskampf*, did exist at the start of the war. Notes from the German handbook of 1939 were subsequently translated and distilled by US Military Intelligence as *German Notes on Street Fighting*, receiving restricted circulation in the series *Tactical and Technical Trends*.

Ideally, towns were to be surrounded and water, power and gas supplies cut off. The object of the attack was to divide the built-up area 'into as many pockets as possible', so denying the enemy freedom of movement. Forces were to advance in the same direction, along parallel streets, where possible capturing buildings with commanding positions. Flanking attacks and moving in different directions were both generally to be avoided, to prevent confused 'friendly fire' incidents. Infantry units were best pushed forward along both sides of streets, keeping close to houses, while others went across roofs and from house to house. Men on one side of the street could cover their comrades by watching roofs, windows and crossings, and where stubborn points of resistance were encountered light machine guns would be moved up for direct fire. Buildings could be destroyed, but weapons of less than 15cm calibre were unsuited to the task; tanks were not to be brought into towns. Once secured, areas were to be systematically searched.

Stubbornly held buildings might be treated just the same as any other fortification, by special 'assault detachments'. Such units (as described in *German Infantry in Action: Minor Tactics*) would be assembled from 'men selected for their courage, determination and physical fitness', led by an 'experienced platoon commander'. These detachments, in the spirit of the Sturmbataillone of the Great War, would employ a selection of suitable weapons, though their personal equipment was pared back to the minimum to ensure mobility. The detachment was organized in several parties according to task, e.g. for breaching wire, destroying weapon embrasures, releasing smokescreens, and delivering supporting fire.[1] In the event these German assault detachments would prove both successful and influential, being emulated by most armies (although the Soviets retrospectively claimed to have invented them).

Where German forces were on the defensive, the best plan was not to reinforce the perimeter, where only a few strongpoints would be established, but to locate mainly within the town where their positions could be concealed. Particularly important buildings were not defended from within but from outside their walls – enemy bombardment of a key structure would thus not endanger many of its defenders. Once an enemy assault was launched, German troops would attempt to turn the tables by splitting attacking units into pockets, and destroying advanced elements by counter-attacks on the flanks. In preparing individual

---

[1] See Elite 160, *World War II Infantry Assault Tactics*

buildings the drill was to open all the windows and create loopholes by removing tiles from the roof. Defenders fired from well back inside rooms, as well as sniping from roofs and behind chimneys. Barricades were well covered by fire, but remotely, from concealed positions. If power supplies were maintained then streets were to remain well illuminated at night, thus making surprise attack difficult.

Individual farms or other isolated buildings required rather different treatment, as described in *Der Feuerkampf der Schutzenkompanie* (1940). In this instance the best plan was for a squad to be placed in cover a few yards to the rear of the structure while the leader adopted an inconspicuous forward observation position, for example lying in the garden. Once enemy troops came into view the rest of the squad could quickly be signalled up into defensive positions in and around the house. In this way the enemy would be fooled into thinking the building was undefended until it was too late, when their own men were exposed to fire at disadvantage.

German close assault detachment attacking a blockhouse with a 1935 model 'Kleif' flamethrower. The NCO squad leader in the foreground carries a *Leucht Pistole*, whose primary use was to fire signal flares; however, it could also be used to ignite fuel containers being used as improvised incendiary weapons during attacks on fortifications and buildings. (Private collection)

British doctrine

The initial British conception, like the German, was that street fighting was essentially undesirable. As *Infantry Section Leading* (1938) explained, 'Street and house to house fighting is always difficult for the attacker, and success will depend largely on the initiative of section commanders.' Street fighting was not considered as the main point of an assault, but as something to be undertaken when 'mopping up' following an attack. In the event of an advance through a village, troops were recommended to adopt the right-hand side of the road as safest, since right-handed riflemen in houses would find it more difficult to fire on them without showing themselves. Wherever possible a light machine gun should be positioned in a window or on a roof where it could cover the advance of the rest of the section. Formations were varied according to circumstance, but the best plan was to send two scouts out in front of the section to watch windows and roofs, opening fire as soon as any enemy was seen. The last two men of the section were to fulfill a similar function, looking back as they proceeded. If trouble was expected, it might be best to abandon the street altogether, saving potential casualties by going through backyards and gardens.

If a house had to be forced, the primary weapons were the hand grenade and the platoon's 2in mortar. Houses were to be cleared systematically, paying special attention to cellars. Before any entry was made every man in a section had to be aware of his task – any dithering in doorways was to be avoided at all costs.

When defending houses, roof-spaces should be occupied, and doors barricaded, though in such a way as to allow a swift exit in an emergency. Cellars were to be examined for places from which 'fire may be opened on the enemy from an unexpected direction'. Ideally the defenders of one house should be able to cover the entrances of nearby buildings, thus providing mutual support. When time allowed, houses were to be

7

fortified by loopholing, sandbagging of windows, and knocking holes through walls to allow movement between houses and gardens without going into the street itself.

These basic ideas were elaborated by *Army Training Memorandum No.23* (July 1939), which offered specific advice on the defence of villages. The point of the exercise was to produce a scheme of defence which was 'self contained' and 'tank proof', to limit the enemy's opportunities for 'exploitation', and to act as a 'pivot' for any 'counter-attack launched to restore the situation'. In defending villages British troops were advised not to act in a predictable manner; nevertheless, defences were to be planned in advance, and executed in such a way as 'to enforce on the enemy a house to house attack which will cause disorganisation and delay'. Particularly advantageous were heavy MG positions outside the village, and LMGs within which could play havoc with any break-in attempt. The core of the defence would be a 'keep' in the village centre, giving good observation. Buildings right on the front edge of settlement were not much use for defensive positions, since they attracted fire, but might be booby-trapped to good effect. Good solid structures further back were more useful, particularly when strengthened – with the addition of loopholes, internal barricades, and nearby alternative positions.

Organizing village defences effectively required both time and manpower, so it was suggested that labour be divided, falling mainly on the pioneer platoons of the infantry and on the engineers. Pioneer platoons were to be responsible for basic preparations, including mounting LMGs, knocking glass from windows, clearing fields of fire, digging trenches, erecting barbed wire, making roadblocks, laying anti-tank mines, and coping with any flammable materials around the position. Engineers executed technical work: strengthening cellars and building command and observation posts, carrying out demolitions requiring explosives, making intercommunication holes through walls, securing a water supply and installing booby traps. Further observations on booby traps were forthcoming in *Army Training Memorandum No.26* (November 1939), which noted a few enemy tricks used in buildings. These included explosive charges that were detonated 'by stepping on a loose floorboard, or by the action of opening a door, window, cupboard or drawer; by switching on electric light; pulling the plug of a water closet; cutting or tripping over a wire; picking up an attractive souvenir or trinket; removing a heap of rubbish on a road; or lighting a fire in a grate'.

Plans for the defence of houses were given in *Field Engineering* (December 1939). Perhaps because the British front in France was inactive in the first winter of the war, some of the schemes were elaborate and time-consuming. These included shoring up cellars; installing steel plates; blocking doors and windows by means of double skins of corrugated iron or wood that could be in-filled with splinterproof rubble; and creating obstacle zones both close to and at a distance from buildings. These might consist of an apron of barbed wire several feet deep around a house to prevent access to doors and windows, and a similar belt beyond grenade-throwing range (see page 4).

A demonstration attack against fortifications with the German pre-war man-pack flamethrower. The fuel tank held just under 12 litres (3 gals) of light and heavy oils, a sticky and highly flammable mixture. The operator approaches the embrasure from one side, then sends in gouts of flame; burns, or simply fear, might prove effective – if not, thick black smoke and oxygen starvation would disable the guncrew. At top left, another member of the team hangs back, ready to move up following the flame attack. (Private collection)

Not an exercise for troops suffering from vertigo: London Home Guards demonstrate roof-crossing at the double in a bombed-out area of terraced housing. Successfully executed, such a manoeuvre allowed an advance without using exposed streets, and allowed houses to be cleared from the attics downwards. (Imperial War Museum H 20884)

The last British digest of street fighting prior to the German onslaught in the West in May 1940 was contained in *Training in Fieldcraft and Elementary Tactics* (March 1940). Though it is debatable how much impact this had in the limited time available, it was a significant advance, based on short practical lessons. These showed the need for scouting, for advancing close to walls, and for 'rear parties' to deal with any tricky enemy who attempted to emerge behind a friendly group. Significant stress was placed on pre-arranged plans for house clearance: the best model was to use just a handful of men per dwelling, with one or two serving as 'guards' in halls or landings while a 'searcher' and one or more 'cover' men moved from room to room.

1940: anticipating invasion

While the May–June 1940 campaign as a whole was little short of disastrous for the British Expeditionary Force, British troops did make good use of street-fighting and house-defence techniques before the fall of France, especially in the defence of Calais. After Dunkirk the UK was divided into areas separated by fortified 'stop lines' to delay invaders, with the bulk of the regular army kept back as a mobile reserve to parry armoured thrusts. In the case of invasion huge numbers of men would be required to delay enemy advances by employing spoiling tactics, and the Local Defence Volunteers – first raised in May 1940, and later renamed the Home Guard – were one answer to this need.[2]

The control of built-up areas and communication nodes was crucial to this overall plan, so initially the Home Guard was committed to a scheme of 'Defended Localities'. These were what Spanish Civil War veteran Hugh Slater described as 'a complete framework of strongpoints between which, and round which the regular army can manoeuvre'. Relatively few complex, long-range weapons were required, grenades

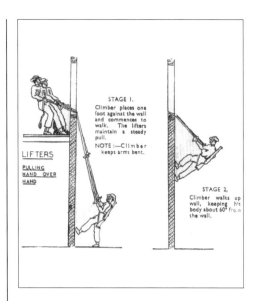

STAGE 1.
Climber places one foot against the wall and commences to walk. The lifters maintain a steady pull.
NOTE :—Climber keeps arms bent.

LIFTERS

PULLING HAND OVER HAND

STAGE 2.
Climber walks up wall, keeping his body about 60° from the wall.

Method for getting troops into upstairs windows by means of the 'fly walk', from Home Guard Instruction No.51, *Battlecraft and Battle Drill for the Home Guard; Part III: Patrolling* (January 1943). The 'lifters' pull the climber up by means of a series of linked toggle ropes.

and incendiary munitions being the key to this type of fighting. As John Brophy's upbeat assessment put it, in his *Home Guard: A Handbook for the LDV* (1940):

> Regular troops cannot be everywhere – but the Home Guard can! In every village, every town and every city of this country there are small formations of local men, a large proportion of them veterans of the last war… The LDV is above all 'the man on the spot'… The general idea is that, wherever enemy troops land, they find themselves trapped in a network of fortified villages and small towns, or suburbs and centres of cities, so that they cannot move in any direction without having to fight. Every such village or other fortified centre will be self contained, and will itself consist of a number of self contained defences organised to resist attack from all directions.

As early as the summer of 1940 Home Guard instructors were teaching the basics of urban combat: keeping out of the street – or, at worst, out of its centre; not bunching; turning corners only with 'the utmost care'; shooting from windows, standing well back inside the room; dropping 'Molotov cocktails' from above; and not manning barricades 'like a trench', but covering them from a flank or nearby buildings. If the men on the spot could report where the Germans were, and delay them even briefly, they would be doing a good job.

Through the efforts of Tom Wintringham, Osterley Park achieved particular fame as a Home Guard battle school, but it was only one of many. Another of the most productive was at Burwash in Sussex, where Maj John Langdon-Davies (another veteran of Spain) addressed 100 battalions between September 1940 and March 1941. Langdon-Davies was also author of the *Home Guard Training Manual,* about 100,000 copies of which were sold by the end of 1941. This contained a thorough section on 'village defence and street fighting'. Among its key recommendations was that villages should be divided into 'outer' and 'inner' defence areas; the defenders of outer roadblocks and covering posts could alert the inner garrison, then fall back if under too much pressure. Near to the centre, though not in an obvious building, would be the 'village stronghold', with well-prepared communications with other parts of the defence. The stronghold was to be concealed, or camouflaged as well as possible; a separate building was to be chosen nearby as the dump for ammunition and petrol. Large villages were best divided into areas, with each zone capable of continuing the fight irrespective of what happened elsewhere.

Major M.D.S. Armour's manual *Total War Training* stated that slit trenches were best placed 50 yards or more from roadblocks, at right angles to the road. So positioned, they gave the best cover to troops who might be attacked by aircraft following the road, and at the same time gave the occupants a good field of fire along it; grenade-throwers could be positioned at the end of the trench nearest to the road. From 1941 the 'Northover Projector' was added to Home Guard arsenals; this grenade-thrower could be used from a concealed position covering a roadblock, being able – as Maj Armour put it – to 'smack up a good blaze with plenty of smoke'. Even more spectacular and dangerous were the simple expedients of flooding dips in a lane with petrol and oil and igniting it, or setting barrels of incendiary mixture to explode or be blown out into the roadway (though naturally such weapons were best used on the approaches to a village rather than within it).

In the event of imminent attack householders had to be prepared to do things 'that no Briton has had to do for centuries': demolish any property that hindered the defence, prepare houses with strengthened walls and ceilings, knock the glass out of windows and cut loopholes; front doors could be barricaded in such a way as to demand explosives to get them open. Good defenders would also try the unorthodox, encompassing minor acts of sabotage such as removing manhole covers at night or cutting communication wires. Buildings could be made to look as though they were strongly defended when they were empty, and dummy mines such as upturned soup-plates could be left in roads – anything that made an advancing enemy hesitate was useful. Stone-throwing, noise-making, misdirection, fake signals and other ruses could all contribute to 'the war of nerves'. (Given the Germans' 70-year-old policy of the harshest reprisals for anything that smacked of *franc-tireur* activity, the cost in civilian lives of following this advice would have been horrific.) Actual street fighting was described in almost playfully up-beat terms as 'the most exciting type of warfare' – the defenders having the advantage, if they started off completely concealed and had perfect knowledge of street plans.

The best Home Guard defence plans were not merely passive, but aggressive whenever the opportunity arose, with counter-attacks made preferably by night. The textbook assault squad was a section of eight men, using shotguns and SMGs wherever available, with phosphorus grenades as an ideal and demoralizing way to screen a rush. Movement was to be silent and unseen, and at irregular intervals: if under enemy MG fire, sections were to wait until the belt had to be changed before making the next dash. Buildings were best cleared from the top downwards, with men standing to one side of a door before opening it; whether opposed or not, it was best for the weapon to enter first and its owner to follow.

An interesting parallel to these 'auxiliary' efforts was Maj Lionel Wigram's publication *Battle School* (1941), a document that was technically unofficial but aimed at regulars, and which was a precursor to the official *Instructors' Handbook on Fieldcraft and Battle Drill* of 1942. The idiosyncratic *Battle School* consciously adopted the best of German techniques, also encouraging a 'battle drill' approach of standard methods taught as a basis for solving tactical problems, to be adapted by trained troops according to

How to turn a small house into an MG post, from Scots Guards Capt S.J. Cuthbert's *We Shall Fight Them in the Streets* (1940). Note that the sandbagged MG position covers the large window from well back, through a loopholed interior room wall. Smaller loopholes for riflemen in prone positions expand the possible angles of fire, and make it unlikely that the enemy can approach the door undetected.

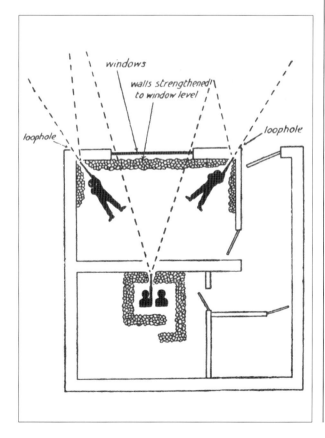

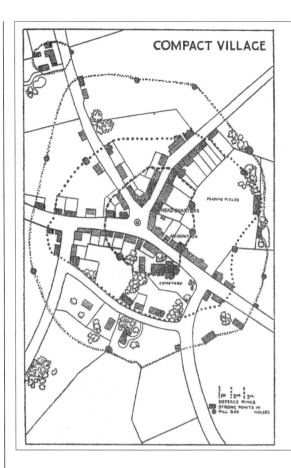

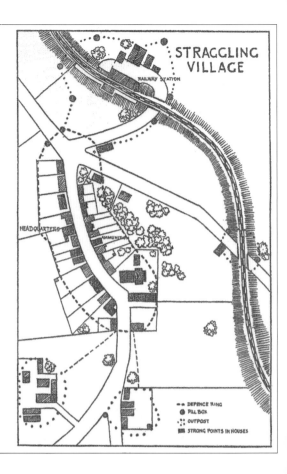

Schemes for the protection of compact and straggling villages, using concentric rings of defence, with pillboxes, outposts and strongpoints in houses, or linked zones of defence. From *Home Guard for Victory* (1941) by the Spanish Civil War veteran Hugh Slater.

Strange as it may sound today, the urban emphasis and 'people's war' flavour of the Home Guard tactical training given by veterans of the Republican army in Spain worried some politicians, whom it reminded of such historical episodes as the Paris Commune of 1871. This was a factor in their seeking to increase links between Home Guard battalions and the regular regiments to which they were soon 'cap-badged'.

circumstances. It was highly influential, especially in the field of urban fighting, since it spelt out some of the earliest versions of house and village clearance drills; these, in improved forms, would ultimately become standard practice throughout the army. Crucial concepts outlined included the use of 'stops' outside villages; the benefit of clearing individual houses from the top downwards; the creation of open 'killing grounds' into which the enemy might be driven; and the use of designated clearing and covering parties for the capture of individual buildings. *Battle School* encouraged infantry movement, both tactically on the battlefield and over longer range by means of buses, as well as pincer movements and the aggressive clearance of various sorts of terrain. Eventually GHQ established an official 'Town Fighting Wing' for the training of urban wafare. Though attendance was far from universal, it would seem that men from virtually every unit in the army were represented on such courses.

By 1942 Home Guard tactical emphasis was likewise moving away from static 'defended localites'; with the arrival of new weapons and the threat of invasion receding, methods were becoming far more 'regular' in character. Nevertheless, street fighting was still regarded as a speciality, and the Home Guard manual *Patrolling* (January 1943) was arguably more advanced and detailed in its coverage than most. Amongst other things it covered urban patrols; movement through houses and sewers, up walls, and over rooftops; the use of streets as 'killing grounds'; 'mouseholing' through walls, and 'ceiling-holing'.

Patrolling also offered standard battle drills for house clearance, of equal standard and clarity to anything taught to the regulars. Interestingly, it was assumed that the Home Guards would still be using mainly US weapons, and the formation for clearing a house was a 'squad' (the American usage), not a 'section' (the standard British term). The eight-man house-searching squad was organized as a Browning Automatic Rifle group and a clearing group; the BAR group was led by the second-in-command, with a two-man gun team and a third rifleman for protection. The squad commander led the clearing group; a 'No.1 bomber' with a shotgun or Sten was his 'personal bodyguard', followed by 'No.1 rifleman – to act as lock side doorman', and 'No.2 bomber', with shotgun or Sten, 'to act as hinge side doorman'. The basic *modus operandi* was for the BAR group to cover as many exits from the target building as possible, while creating a 'killing ground' in the street. The clearing group conducted actual searches, entering through a back door or window.

As they approached the rear of the building the commander and No.1 bomber would cover the advance of the other two men as they crept up through any cover, keeping below the level of windows. The No.1 rifleman and No.2 bomber took positions either side of the most convenient door or window, backs to the wall; the No.1 rifleman then burst open the door, shooting the lock if necessary, and the No.2 bomber threw in a grenade. When the grenade had exploded the commander and No.1 bomber dashed inside past their two comrades, getting their backs against the walls and shooting any enemy discovered. Leaving one man to cover the bottom of the stairs, the other three then went up – No.1 bomber first, followed by No.1 rifleman, followed by the commander. The team then cleared the house, roof downwards, signalling their success to the BAR group when complete. No member of the squad was allowed to enter the designated killing ground until all houses overlooking it had been cleared.

American responses

Though their country was not under any immediate threat, the US authorities' preparations for war definitely extended to fighting in built-up areas. The Marine Corps was perhaps the service most ready for urban combat, but even their doctrine specified that the most likely eventuality was civil unrest among the populations of Third World towns where expeditionary forces might have to intervene. Changing such perceptions was a significant struggle, in which the Corps of Engineers – and notably a Capt Paul W. Thompson – played a leading role. In the months after the fall of France he wrote articles for the *Infantry Journal* in which he pointed out that the 'incontestable' conclusion to be drawn from recent events was that 'intimate co-ordination' between members of the combat team was imperative. Combat engineers were obviously a crucial part of that team, but battlefield engineers of all descriptions were seriously under-represented. In late 1940 and 1941 the US Engineer School therefore formed a series of committees on the subject, and included factors such as road blocks in manoeuvres. It would be some time, however, before thoroughly modern tactics were evolved and could be disseminated through literature and training.

THE EASTERN FRONT, 1941–44

The opening rush

During its first surge eastward in 1941, the Wehrmacht only allowed towns and villages to impede the advance if their capture was vital – for instance, in order to secure a river crossing. Even then many were taken at the run, shock being regarded as more important than preparation. However, whereas in 1939 there had been a general expectation of avoiding committing armour to built-up areas, German tacticians now seemed more ambivalent. A German document on armoured divisions, translated early in 1942, set out the general parameters:

> Except where necessary, tanks should not be employed in built-up areas, since their movements are restricted and they are easy targets for anti-tank weapons. When the armoured division is compelled to fight in a built-up area, the task should be assigned to the motorized infantry… [these] may be strengthened by single heavy tanks, heavy anti-tank guns, and engineer assault detachments [to] give support by engaging particularly strongly fortified defended areas. Built-up areas can be overcome more rapidly and with fewer casualties if smoke is used to blind the enemy, if he is paralyzed by artillery and bombing attacks, or if the area is burned down. Tank and motorized infantry units following in the rear of the first wave will be employed to flank the locality and take it from the rear. Liaison must be insured between forces carrying out the frontal and flank attacks.

How this worked in practice was demonstrated by an account of how a Panzergrenadier company dealt with the village of Krutojarka in the Ukraine. Once action was imminent the company moved at speed in its armoured carriers, dispersed in both width and depth with at least 20 yards between vehicles:

> Guns can be seen flashing at the edge of the village. The Russian force is engaged. We hear the fire of the Russian anti-tank guns and our own tank cannon, and, in between, the sound of both sides' machine gun fire. The Panzergrenadier company commander gives his orders by radio: as soon as the grenadiers see Russian soldiers, they are to fire on them direct from their carriers, or else dismount quickly and fight on the ground… The first tanks enter Krutojarka, but presently reappear. The company commander radios the order 'Clear the town!' The personnel carriers advance past the tanks, which are firing with all their guns, and move towards the edge of the village…
>
> A personnel carrier's track is hit by a flanking anti-tank gun. The grenadiers jump out and assault the gun crew with machine-gun fire, while the driver and the man beside him get out and, under fire, change the link of the broken track. The attacking grenadiers have now reached a street at the edge of the village. Startled by the suddenness of the assault, the Russians take cover in houses, bunkers, foxholes and other hideouts. The grenadiers jump out of the carriers and advance along the street, making good

Boys building a typical barricade in the streets of Odessa at the time of the 1941 siege. For its staunch resistance the Black Sea port was eventually elevated to the Soviet status of 'Hero City', along with Moscow, Leningrad, Stalingrad and Kiev. Similar street barricades would be erected by the Polish Home Army during the Warsaw rising of August–October 1944.

use of grenades, pistols and bayonets. The driver and the second man remain in each carrier. The carriers skirt around the sides of the village, with the men beside the drivers delivering flanking fire against the buildings. Soon the roofs of the houses are on fire; the smoke grows thicker and thicker. Three tanks push forward along the main street to support the attack of the grenadiers.

We find the smoke an advantage, as it prevents the Russians discovering that there are relatively few of us. Also, as a result of the poor visibility, the Russians cannot employ their numerous machine guns with full effect. We, for our part, are able to engage in the close fighting in which we excel. It is no longer possible to have one command for the company; officers and NCOs have formed small shock detachments, which advance from street corner to street corner, and from bunker to ditch, eliminating one Russian nest after another. A lieutenant holds a grenade until it almost explodes, and then throws it into a bunker…

As explained in the British *Periodical Notes on the German Army*, where villages lay in the path of an armoured division it was the job of the lorried or armoured infantry to clear them, 'engineers armed with explosives and flamethrowers' giving valuable support. While fire against the outskirts – supplemented by generated smoke or burning buildings – occupied the defenders from various quarters, the main attack came in from 'an unexpected direction'. The hard slog was then the job of dismounted troops, 'organized for street fighting', commonly using 'one company with support weapons under command' concentrated to deal with a row of houses. Where resistance was stiff it might be necessary to use as much as a battalion with attached troops for a single street.

As the German offensive faltered in the East the whole campaign became less of a *Sichelschnitt* ('sickle cut') through the opposition, and much more a matter of 'take and hold'. Protracted fighting in built-up areas was a symptom of this change, and it is arguable that extensive street fighting was one of the first signs of German failure in the East. Urban battles cost large numbers of men, and in comparison with Germany the USSR's human resources appeared almost limitless. Many towns would be fought over during four years of war, notably Orel, Odessa, Zhitomir, Rostov, Kharkov, Sevastopol and finally Berlin itself; but one battle for a city naturally stands out, and it was during the struggle for Stalingrad that Russian street-fighting methods would be immeasurably improved.

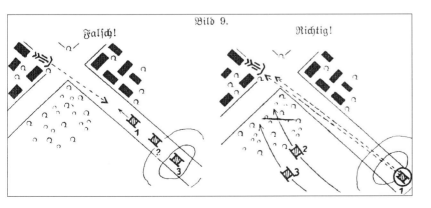

German diagram illustrating the correct armoured approach to a built-up area. As soon as resistance is encountered Tank 1 takes whatever cover is available (in this case retreating to a hull-down position behind a rise), while Tanks 2 & 3 manoeuvre to outflank the AT gun under the covering fire of Tank 1.

15

German 1941 model flamethrower; at 18kg (40lb) this weapon was considerably lighter than its predecessors, but still a burden. Its ignition system featured a heated wire at the muzzle of the projector tube. It could project five bursts to a range of about 30 yards, the heat of the flame reaching up to 800°C. (Private collection)

STALINGRAD: THE ACADEMY OF STREET FIGHTING

The street fighting in Stalingrad was remarkable not just for its scale, but for its variety. Not only did the opponents have to fight for buildings of every conceivable size and shape, but their materials degraded in different ways to produce very different combat landscapes. Flimsy workers' cottages provided almost no cover from bullets, and when bombed or burnt they disintegrated to nothing much more than a brick chimney left standing like a tree. Modern factories might be blasted so thoroughly as to lose their roofs and floors, but their walls of reinforced concrete were so tough that explosions tended to be directed upwards, leaving linear bulwarks across the battlefield. In the city centre sewers and basements provided a subterranean dimension – what the Germans dubbed the *Rattenkrieg* ('rat warfare'). On the outskirts the landscape could be flat, or might be seamed with *balkas* – ravines, in which whole units might be completely concealed. Hills dominated certain sectors, and offered secure positions from which the Germans sometimes dominated the vital traffic of supplies and replacements from the Soviet-held east bank of the Volga. Just north of the city centre was the Mamayev Kurgan (Mamayev Hill) – an old Tartar burial mound, also known as Height 102. Nikolai Maznitsa of the Soviet 95th Rifle Division first saw it in mid September 1942, and even then it was 'completely covered in corpses. In some places you had to move two or three bodies to lie down. They quickly began to decompose, and the stench was appalling.' Even after the war the hill was so poisoned with shrapnel and debris that no grass would grow for some time.

Russian tactics in the early summer fighting were far from sophisticated. New formations were poured across the Volga, running the gauntlet of air strikes and artillery with precious little modern equipment, and less tactical training. Famously, some units even went into battle with one rifle between two men, in the hope that one would survive to pick up the weapon if his comrade fell. The Soviet stance was governed above all by Stavka Order No.227, signed personally by Stalin, which dictated that there would be 'Not one step back'; any 'panickers and cowards' were 'to be eliminated on the spot', while officers ordering unauthorized retreats would be considered 'traitors to the Motherland'.

Chuikov's Order No.166

Russian methods improved perceptibly as the battle progressed. A tactical landmark was Order No.166, issued by Gen Chuikov of 62nd Army at the end of September. This concluded with the sound advice to subordinate commanders that operations were not to be carried out by 'whole units like companies and battalions. The offensive should be organized chiefly on the basis of small groups, with sub-machine guns, hand grenades, bottles of incendiary mixture and anti-tank rifles. Regimental and battalion artillery should be used to support attacking groups by firing point blank into windows, embrasures and attics.' As Chuikov's memoirs observed, this meant that only portions of each battalion were committed at any one time, in 'storm groups' on limited sectors, while other troops remained on the defensive.

Storm-group actions were commonly initiated at night, so that troops could creep as close as possible under cover of darkness before rushing across any open ground; this 'stealthy approach' might bring the Russians to within 30 yards or less of their target. Storm groups comprised three elements: assault sections, reinforcement groups, and reserves. The precise strength and composition of these varied according to the task and the fruits of reconnaissance. In gathering intelligence the assault commander was to consider such factors as the type of building to be attacked; the thickness of walls and floors; the presence of any cellar; entrances and exits; types of fortification and embrasures; and the defenders' communication links with supporting forces. With such information it was possible to determine the defenders' strengths and fields of fire, modifying the attacking force and direction of attack accordingly. Typical arrangements, based on actual organizations used by Guards units during attacks on the so-called 'L-Shaped House', were described as follows:

> The basis of the storm group was the assault groups, containing between six and eight men in each. They would first of all swiftly break into the building and wage battle independently within it. Each group had its own part of the overall task to carry out. These groups were lightly armed, [each man] carrying an SMG, grenades, a dagger and an entrenching tool [often used as a hatchet]. The groups were under one commander, who had signal rockets and flares, and sometimes a [field] telephone.
>
> The reinforcement group was normally divided into separate parties, which would enter the building from different directions immediately after the assault groups (as soon as the commander gave the signal 'We're in!'). After entering the building and seizing the firing positions, they rapidly developed their own fire against the enemy, to prevent any attempts to come to the assistance of his beleaguered garrison. This group was equipped with heavier weapons: heavy machine guns, mortars, anti-tank rifles and AT guns, crowbars, picks and explosives. Each group contained sappers, snipers and soldiers of various trades…

German 1942 model flamethrower, ultimately the commonest variant in the arsenal. Improvements in this type included a shorter projection tube, and more reliable ignition by means of a 9mm blank cartridge system – the original device often failed in the extreme cold of the first Russian winter. By March 1944 production had reached 4,000 units a month, and it was supplied not only to the Heer but to the Luftwaffe, Kriegsmarine and some Polizei units. A very light 'people's' or '46' model flamethrower was also produced for the Volkssturm in the last months of the war. (Private collection)

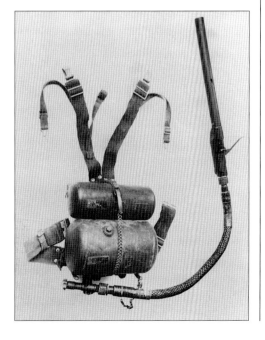

German infantrymen shelter behind a wall in Stalingrad, late autumn 1942; note two junior NCOs, identifiable by their distinctive collar-edge lace. The men in the foreground are probably the commander and the LMG team of the Gruppe or squad. Visible weapons include at least one MP40, an MG34, and grenades thrust into belts. (IWM HU 5131)

The reserve group was to be used to supplement and strengthen the assault groups, to stop any possible enemy attack from the flanks, and also (if need be) as a blocking party. The reserve group could [also] be employed for the rapid creation ... of additional assault groups.

Experience suggested that forming the storm group from one parent unit was the best policy, giving cohesion and flexibility. The jumping-off point was to be as close to the enemy as possible; while this meant an almost constant duel with enemy infantry, it also made German use of aircraft and heavy weapons in close support almost impossible. Individual members of the leading assault groups were advised to creep up through shellholes and ruins, sometimes on all fours, with SMGs and up to a dozen grenades. One or more of these was generally used during the advance to contact, and indeed the length of the grenade-throw often predetermined the distance of the final attack. This would become Chuikov's so-called 'hand grenade rule', a frequently cited tactical maxim from the Stalingrad battle: not to move without throwing a grenade first, and to move no further in one bound than a grenade could be thrown – i.e., about 25 yards.

Once inside a house the basic drill was to throw a grenade into each room, entering it as soon as possible thereafter – 'fighting inside a building is always frantic'. Timing and surprise were crucial to success. In some instances, as at the 'Railwayman's House', this meant the launching of the storm group attack hard on the heels of an artillery and machine-gun barrage, while the Germans were still reeling. At the 'L-Shaped House' there was no preparatory fire to telegraph the moment of the attack; the Guardsmen commenced the assault from close range, tossing grenades through windows and bursting in after the explosions. Where there was no barrage *per se*, it might still be possible to use a single small-calibre gun, 'brought up at night or under cover of a smokescreen', to neutralize enemy positions or to prevent fresh troops being fed in. Another more elaborate option, requiring extensive planning, was to co-ordinate the attack with full-blown mining operations, in which sappers would tunnel under the enemy, with or without the aid of existing sewers, and blow up all or part of his position.

Reinforcement group orders were also adapted according to circumstance, but a typical sequence was given thus:
(1) Machine gunners, AT riflemen and mortar crews enter the building first with their weapons, followed by their assistants carrying enough ammunition and rations for a day's fighting.
(2) Having entered the building, the men immediately occupy the centre or upper floors, so as to be able to cover the surrounding area and prevent enemy reserves from coming up.

(3) After occupying and equipping the firing points ... the group organizes additional firing points at the approaches – in front and at the flanks (to enable further active operations to take place).

(4) After taking possession of the building, the group ... must rapidly make communication trenches, adapt blockhouses and build new ones. There is no point in just settling down in the building; you have to persistently try to get closer to the enemy.

Soviet storm group tactics were infinitely better than some of the crude 'human waves' that had preceded them, but any impression given that they were a tactical innovation was spurious. Very similar methods had been outlined by the Germans as early as 1939, and indeed some of the tactics used in attacking trench systems and bunkers as early as 1916 contained comparable elements. We should also note that post-war statistical analysis suggests that the Russians actually lost more troops than the Germans during the battle for Stalingrad.

Soviet offensive directives were complemented by Order No.171 of 28 September 1942, which specified defensive measures, including both tank and infantry obstacles 'in depth', and the preparation of buildings:

> In building obstacles all resources available on the spot should be used, even dismantling buildings and taking up tramlines, bringing up the civilian population to help in the work through local organizations. The main work should be carried out by the units themselves ... by night and day...

As Chuikov later explained, the basic defensive position was the 'centre of resistance', comprising a number of strongpoints. The best were of stone and brick, not merely because they were stronger, but because they were less likely to be set alight (indeed, some of the best had already been burned out once, which tended to reduce future fire risk). Ideally the structures within the centre of resistance were linked with trenches, and the gaps between the buildings were swept

German postcard from the series 'Our Waffen-SS', showing 'a fight in a built-up area in the East'. An MG34 fires from a pile of rubble up a gap between buildings – the classic LMG tactic in support of infantry clearing houses – while covered by a cautious rifleman.

In one of the best-known images of Stalingrad, Russian infantrymen shelter among the ruins while they take a brief snack, guarded by one of the squad's two M1928 Degtyarev DP light machine guns. The other *frontoviki* are armed for maximum firepower, with two PPSh-41 sub-machine guns, and (right) an SVT-40 semi-automatic rifle.

by fire and blocked with obstructions. Individual strongpoints might be held by any number of men, from a squad to a battalion, but as far as possible they were adapted for all-round defence, and could wage battle independently for several days.

Different levels of multi-storied buildings were suitable for different types of defence. Infantrymen with grenades and light automatic weapons could be positioned almost anywhere, but basement and lower floor embrasures were especially suitable for heavy weapons such as artillery, AT guns and HMGs firing along streets. These also did useful work as flanking weapons, emplaced outside and behind buildings. Upper floors and attics were best for light AT weapons, riflemen, observers, and machine guns for engaging more distant targets and enemy hidden nearby. Both sides made extensive use of booby traps and anti-personnel mines.

As the months of fighting progressed more tanks became available, and where these were disabled they were seldom recovered for repair, but used as stationary pillboxes behind the front lines, to ambush any German armour venturing deep into the position. Defence against armour included not only the close-range use of AT rifles and guns, but the full arsenal of standard and improvised incendiaries and charges. Both sides learned to attack armour from above – and preferably from close in, so that the tank's main gun would be unable to elevate sufficiently to reply. Mines and roadblocks prevented retreat when laid behind enemy armour.

Pavlov's House and the Black House

Individual buildings took on not merely tactical but mythological propaganda significance, notably the Red October and Barrikady factories, the Univermag department store, and the castle-like 'grain elevator'. The celebrated Stalingradsky Traktony Zavod or Tractor Works had long since been converted to tank production, and during the early stages of the battle unpainted T-34s, still lacking inessential components, drove off the production line straight into action. The staff and students of the Stalingrad Technical University not only provided manpower for digging defences, but formed the nucleus of a grandly named 'destroyer battalion'.

Perhaps the most famous building of all was the small apartment block known as 'Pavlov's House', so called because it was first recaptured in September, without a fight, by just four men led by Sgt Yakov Pavlov – a story reported at length in Red Army newspapers. The block overlooked Ninth of January Square, and stuck out into the German lines like a salient, thus attracting constant fire and frequent assaults. Pavlov's men were not alone for long, being joined by an officer and reinforcements who blocked up vulnerable openings using bricks and boxes of sand, occupied the roof and the basement with its thick supporting walls, and installed not only machine guns but an AT gun.

Hammering from German heavy weapons eventually caused the floors of Pavlov's House to begin to collapse one upon another, and many of the garrison were killed, but the position did not become weaker. Mines were placed surreptitiously around the building, and fresh troops approached under cover of darkness, being fed up from 'the Mill' – a more secure spot a few hundred yards to the rear. At one point, according to Soviet sources, the defenders were reduced to just one working SMG supplemented by the last few grenades, and bricks. General Chuikov boasted that the enemy lost more men attacking Pavlov's House than they did in taking Paris. (Rather less well publicized was the fact that after the war a traumatized Pavlov eventually became an Orthodox monk.)

The 'Black House' was less well known, and one of the last points to be retaken by the Russians, but it was a similar essay in close combat in a built-up area. Ivan Vakurov of the 173rd Rifles would recall:

> The storming of the house began in the morning, after an artillery bombardment. The Germans, hiding behind the thick stone walls, were firing from all the windows and out of the basement. The storm groups moved forward in short hops, covering each other's approach with gunfire. Lieutenant Rostovtsev was first to get into the doorway of the Black House. Using grenades and machine guns, we carved out a path up to the stairs. Right behind Rostovtsev were Lt Titov, Sgt Khoroshev, Zapolyansky and Matveyev. There was a struggle on the staircase landing at the second floor, and an enemy bullet felled Lt Rostovtsev; Sgt Zhernov took his place. While the battle continued on the second floor, more storm groups burst into the building. There were battles in every corner of the house. Khoroshev covered Matveyev as he climbed up into the attic, and attached the flag to the chimney stack.

Like buildings, snipers became the subject of propaganda, producing a 'sniper cult'. Published individual 'kill' totals ranged above 200, but snipers in general did make a significant contribution, not only in terms of attrition but in undermining enemy morale and limiting movement. Intelligence, caution, fieldcraft and prediction were significant urban sniping skills and, since ranges were usually short, were of greater significance than simple marksmanship. Key tactics included the use of multiple firing positions, dummy decoy figures, movement by night, and unusual 'hides' such as pipes and camouflaged eyries.[3]

A German weapons pit during the battle for a Stalingrad suburb, autumn 1942. Some of the nearby wooden buildings have been all but swept away by bombs and shellfire, leaving the two-man pit by far the most secure position. Its occupants man both an MG34 LMG and a 5cm light mortar, and an MP38 SMG is laid ready on the plank shelf. A heap of empty MG ammunition boxes (left foreground) is mute evidence of recent fierce fighting. (IWM HU 5140)

[3] See Elite 68, *The Military Sniper since 1914*

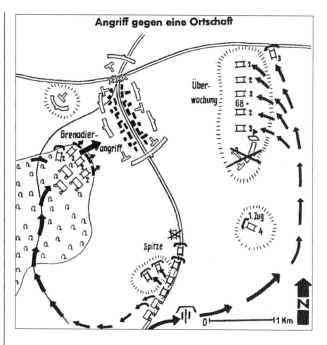

German manual diagram of the ideal attack against a prepared village, featuring a full-blown armour and Panzergrenadier assault. As the *Spitze* or point of the column (low centre) comes under fire the surviving lead tanks take cover. Part of the remaining armour sweeps around well to the right of the village, remaining under cover of contours at least 1km (1,000 yards) away from the enemy; they succeed in overrunning an enemy position atop a rise, and go into 'overwatch' ready to give covering fire. The bulk of the Panzergrenadiers, escorted by the remaining tanks, form the left jaw of the 'pincers', driving through a wood. At the edge closest to the village they dismount to launch an all-out attack under cover of the guns of the Panzers.

WARSAW: IMPROVISATION AND TERROR

Some of the most merciless street fighting in the East was in Warsaw, where there were two distinct bouts of combat before the belated entry of the Red Army. In April 1943, Jewish fighters attempted to resist the liquidation of the Ghetto; the defenders mustered no more than a few hundred firearms – most no heavier than pistols – for a brave stand lasting nearly three weeks before the Waffen-SS crushed all opposition. Most of the surviving Jews were then transported to the extermination camp at Treblinka. The second episode, the great 'Warsaw Rising' of August 1944, was undertaken in the hope that the city could be freed before the imminent arrival of the Soviets – thus both weakening the German war effort, and placing the Polish Home Army in its liberated capital on a stronger footing with regard to the advancing Red Army.

The Home Army and other smaller resistance groups could muster about 50,000 covert soldiers, but there was a dire shortage of arms. Weapons were initially estimated at about 3,000 rifles, pistols and SMGs; 35 anti-tank weapons, including several British PIATs; 25,000 hand grenades (many of them locally made *filipinkis*); and just seven machine guns. Additional armament was dropped in by the RAF, captured from the enemy, or manufactured in clandestine workshops, so that eventually almost half the potential strength of the Home Army had some form of weapon. Witold Gorski, a 16-year-old volunteer, was later to recall that the bulk of the guns went to experienced men – youngsters made do with Molotov cocktails. The immediate German garrison of just over 10,000, under Gen Rainer Stahel, was outnumbered at the outset, but many more troops were rapidly drawn in. These included not just Battle Group Rohr and SS-Battle Group Reinefarth with the ghastly SS-Assault Bde Dirlewanger, but large numbers of *Ost* troops: renegade Russians, Ukrainians including the infamous Kaminski Bde, Cossacks and Azeris, and various Police and Security battalions.

The Polish commander, Gen Antoni Chrusciel, divided the city into eight areas. His strategy was well-suited to a partisan army with primitive communications and limited firepower: to seize the city centre, cut communication and supply routes, and hold out by means of barricades and street fighting for the few days that it was anticipated Rokossovsky's 1st Belorussian Front – whose first guns could be heard to the east – would need to relieve Warsaw. The first phase, begun on 1 August 1944, was to move units secretly into key positions before suddenly opening fire. The leadership was later criticized for starting the battle in broad daylight, but whether command and control would have been possible in darkness is questionable. Julian Kulski's platoon was just one of many that walked to their positions with pistols and Sten guns hidden under their jackets:

At that moment, a German patrol truck drove quite slowly down Krasinski Street. Seeing the column, the Germans brought the vehicle to a screeching halt and opened fire on the men in the middle of the boulevard. Swida responded with his Sten gun; one of his men pulled a light machine gun out of a sack, took up position and, after firing a short salvo, uttered a curse: his gun was stuck. At that moment Wilk and Horodenski entered the action. The Germans, surprised by fire on their flank … turned round. This gave the opportunity to the Swida group to withdraw to Kochowska Street. The firing was still fierce, and bullets whined over our heads as we lay flat in the green centre strip dividing the boulevard. I kept firing back, Wilk wounded a couple more of them with his Sten gun, and the Germans withdrew.

While the Poles captured most of their objectives in the city centre, Old Town and Wola – as well as several armoured vehicles and Panzerfaust AT weapons – some isolated strongpoints remained. At the PAST (state telephone) building a party of Germans was besieged for three weeks, with the Poles attempting to dislodge them floor by floor, until the Kilinski Bn took drastic action. Female sappers – so-called *minerki* – detonated explosives in the basement, and home-made flamethrowers were used. Many Germans were killed or leapt from windows, and 115 were captured.

However, in many suburbs, including Praga in the east, the insurrection was unsuccessful; the Vistula bridges could not be held, and attacks on Okecie airfield failed. Soon, with German reinforcements arriving – and massacring the civilian inhabitants out of hand, or using them as human shields – the Home Army was gradually constrained within the central area. Here they were battered with Luftwaffe bombs, and bombarded with heavy weapons including Nebelwerfers. These hated rocket launchers were christened 'musical boxes' or 'bellowing cows': a poster warned Varsovians, 'When the cow bellows, don't stand in the doorway!'. One who survived their fury only by a miracle was Zdzislaw Jarkiewicz of the Gustaw-Harnas Battalion:

Just then, a deafening explosion of a direct hit on our location tore through the air turning me into a lit torch. Instinctively, I rolled on the ground to put out the flames and ripped off my shirt. The scorched remains of my uniform fell to the ground. Half naked and mad with pain I ran stumblingly to the first aid station … I felt pain, terrible pain. I glanced at my jelly-like arms. I caught my image in the wall mirror and froze, not recognizing myself. Burned face. No hair. Swollen eyes. The frame of my glasses twisted from the heat – but amazingly, they had saved my eyesight. I looked horrible. But I was alive!

Close support from armoured assault guns also formed an integral part of German tactics: as the US *Intelligence Bulletin* of December 1944 reported:

The use of the concentrated charge – several grenade-heads wired around a complete stick grenade – against an enemy-held house. This move, very effective if successful, required the thrower to survive long enough to get very close to his target. From a series of German wartime postcards depicting the role of the infantry.

INFANTERIE GREIFT AN!
Mit geballter Ladung bekämpft der Grenadier seinen Gegner.

German squad leaders being briefed by their officer during the battle for Stalingrad, 1942. The man on the left, wearing a greatcoat, has a captured Soviet SVT-40 semi-automatic rifle. Lacking radio communication at squad and platoon level, the infantry needed careful advanced co-ordination with supporting fire units if small-unit assaults in built-up areas were to succeed.

In attacks on fortified towns and villages, assault guns advance by batteries. Their mission is to destroy the foremost houses. After the infantry has broken into the edge of the town or village, the guns of the battery split up, and, by previous arrangement, join the various infantry-engineer assault groups and fight with them. In village and street fighting, assault guns are considered most useful in breaking up road blocks, barricades and fortified houses … assault guns also provide direct fire against embrasures, and other vulnerable points, of fortified positions. In missions of this type they work with infantry-engineer teams seeking to break into the hostile position.

As the Germans sliced Warsaw into ever smaller islands, fighters attempted to escape the trap. Many, like Cpl Karol Tomaszewski of the Baszta Regt, took to the sewers:

Female liaison officers served as sewer guides; these women had traversed the sewers repeatedly carrying orders and munitions. At first we had to proceed on all fours, but then we were able to stand erect. It was the later part of September and the waste water flowing through the sewers was cold. In some places the Germans had managed to dam the flow of the water with ready-made barriers which we had to breach and allow the water to ebb before being able to proceed. At such times the water reached our chins. We had to observe strict silence and could hear the Germans shouting through manholes suggesting we come up and surrender, but I later learned that those who did were promptly shot. And so it went on for eleven long hours. I had been lucky to have received a bottle of vodka before entering the sewer … when I found myself weakening and shivering, I would lean against the side of the tunnel and take a drink. I emerged totally exhausted, smelly and befouled.

Despite broadcasting demands for the Polish rising, the Soviets effectively left the Home Army to its fate, though this was not as cynical as has been suggested; Rokossovsky's reconnaissance spearhead from the east was pushed back 25 miles by fierce German counter-attacks. The Western Allies air-dropped equipment, at great risk and hampered by Soviet obstructionism, but this did little more than prolong the agony. After 63 days all resistance ceased on 4 October, brutally suppressed by troops supported by tanks, artillery and aircraft. The Germans and their jackals had suffered about 17,000 fatalities, and well over 200,000 Poles had died – the great majority of them the civilian victims of casual massacre and mass executions (Dirlewanger and Kaminski are reckoned to have murdered some 10,000 in Wola on 5 August alone). Following systematic burning and repeated air raids and shelling, it was estimated that 85 per cent of the city had been destroyed, including 923 historic buildings, almost 150 schools, two universities and the national library. The contrast with Paris, liberated in late August, could not have been greater. There a French rising had been rapidly supported by the arrival of American and Free French forces, and the German commander ignored belated orders to raze the city, most of which survived.

German analysis

Nevertheless, the suppressors of the 1944 Warsaw Uprising were by no means completely satisfied with their performance. Armoured tactics came in for particular criticism, and were addressed in a document entitled *Notes for Panzer Troops*, which was later captured and translated by US Intelligence. This was supposed to be a model for future urban battles that included tanks, and ten crucial points were stressed:

(1) That unco-ordinated heavy support weapons were ineffective. The remedy was to concentrate resources on 'approved targets', with the infantry ready to react 'as soon as the last shell has fallen'. The role of armour with infantry would then be to use suppressive fire to prevent enemy intervention during the attack.

(2) That there had been too much use of open streets by German troops. In future progress was to be primarily through house walls, by which means wounded and ammunition could also be moved out of view.

(3) In future all captured buildings would be consolidated as a matter of course, with windows and other openings turned into firing ports. Entrances and stairs to cellars should be the subject of special attention, while any subterranean passages which could not immediately be cleared were to be barricaded, or blown in and guarded, with no troops allowed to 'stand round idly'.

(4) Contrary to popular perception, completely ruined buildings continued to be of use to the enemy: therefore even rubble had to be occupied or covered by fire. Patrols would be mounted to ferret out any hostile stragglers.

(5) Random destruction was often counter-productive, so in future only outbuildings affording the enemy covered approach to vital points would be destroyed as a matter of course.

(6) Using tanks as bulldozers against walls and

Warsaw, October 1944: under the eyes of a German Police officer, Gen Bor-Komorowski, one of the Polish resistance leaders, surrenders to SS-Gen Erich von dem Bach-Zelewski following the crushing of the uprising. Bor's grudging handshake was doubtless calculated to help save the lives of as many of his men as possible. (IWM MH 4489)

barricades made them vulnerable to close-range AT weapons. In future attacks on barricades and obstacles, the infantry was to approach first to force a passage, with 'squads of civilians' to be 'put to work to complete the clearing of debris' later.

(7) Failure to use rifles to full effect proved a false economy. In future, rifle and machine-gun fire must be delivered promptly and steadily from all newly captured buildings. Rifle fire is concentrated on group targets to keep the enemy's heads down. The enemy is not given a moment's rest, but feels himself perpetually observed and engaged. Rapid opening of fire is especially important to avoid giving the enemy time to withdraw to alternate positions.

(8) The attackers had not exploited the civilian population to its fullest potential[!]. The remedy was to ensure that able-bodied inhabitants should be used to clear debris; 'the German army must enforce this point relentlessly, even when the work is performed under fire'.

(9) More cunning methods are required to counter the enemy, with tricks, such as feints employed to draw fire and to silence it.

(10) Poor communications jeopardized efficiency: therefore assault detachments are to be better instructed in co-operation, fire and movement, with reports both to and from attacking units to keep them informed.

As a rider to these basic points the Inspector General of Panzer Troops observed that 'when tanks are used in street fighting, they should be employed like the so-called "tank-infantry teams" used in Normandy, – that is, small infantry units will be detailed to cooperate directly with tanks. To reduce casualties, four main principles would be adhered to: no splitting of forces; thorough and purposeful concentration of fire; immediate infantry exploitation of tank fire; and close mutual support throughout.

German paratroopers of 1.Fallschirmjäger Div take up positions among the ruins of Cassino town. Both sides learned that destruction of buildings and the expulsion of a determined enemy were not the same thing in urban warfare. (Count E.G.Vitetti Collection)

THE ITALIAN EXPERIENCE

Though Western Allied troops fought in North Africa and elsewhere, it was only with the invasion of Italy that sustained street fighting became a common feature of their battle experience, leading to the revision of existing doctrine and publication of new manuals. For the 1st Canadian Division the fighting in Ortona on the Adriatic coast in December 1943 was a rite of passage: a three-week battle which the press, with some exaggeration, dubbed 'a second Stalingrad'. The German paratroopers defending the town certainly proved remarkably skilful, as was later described by a Canadian officer for a US *Intelligence Bulletin*:

The defensive layout was based on an intimate knowledge of the town, the approaches, the alleyways, and the best routes from street to street, building to building, and even room to room. With this detailed knowledge, the enemy sited his weapons and carried out a determined defence, the

outstanding feature of which was acknowledged by our troops to have been 'sheer guts'. The enemy had chosen a 'killing ground', and all his weapons were sited to cover this area. Where the approaches to the 'killing ground' could not be covered by fire, the Germans had demolished buildings so as to create debris obstacles. The enemy could, and did, cover these obstacles by fire. Groups of machine guns were always sited so that the fire of one supported the fire of another.[4]

The mountainous heaps of rubble left by the Allied bombing and shelling of Cassino town hampered attempts to get New Zealand tanks forward in close support of their infantry. (IWM NA 13800)

Anti-tank guns were cleverly camouflaged in the ruins and positioned to enfilade tank routes. Linking tunnels provided swift movement within the position, while attackers were harassed by snipers, grenade-throwers and the surprise use of a flamethrower. Though actual counter-attacks were lacking, German troops filtered back into any captured areas left undefended, and would replace incapacitated garrisons with fresh troops anything up to four times during the fight. (There were also some largely unprofitable sorties by Focke-Wulf Fw 190 ground attack aircraft.)

The eight-day fight of the Loyal Edmonton Regt is recorded in its War Diary. During this time the battalion pressed along the main street of the town, clearing buildings either side, to create a passage for supporting armour. Though tank guns at close range did 'excellent work' in neutralizing enemy fire, the fighting strength of the unit was reduced to just three companies of 60 men apiece by Christmas Eve. Even so, by Boxing Day the Edmontons had penetrated as far as Cathedral Square. Here they discovered that the enemy had planted charges, one of which was detonated and buried an entire Canadian platoon; rescuers

---

[4] See Elite 122, *World War II Infantry Tactics: Company and Battalion*, Plate D

A waste of precious heavy armour – a German PzKw V Panther disabled during street fighting. Though howitzer-armed AFVs and engineer tanks did have roles to play, cramped streets were seldom suitable for the employment of long-range flat-trajectory tank guns, and if insufficient infantry was provided to protect tanks they could easily fall prey to infantry AT weapons. This early Panther Ausf D, faintly marked 'red 102' and probably from the re-formed 16.Pz Div (already wiped out once, in the streets of Stalingrad) has a tow-cable attached for attempted recovery: the turret is rotated to '6 o'clock'.

How the 'ambidextrous marksman' changes hands to make the best use of cover in urban combat – from D. Whipp's *Street and Guerilla Fighting* (1942). Note also how the rifleman stands well back when shooting from a window; the generous wall of sandbags presupposes that his section have had a lot of time to prepare the house for defence.

burrowing into the rubble succeeded in releasing four men, while a 3in mortar 'stonk' of 1,100 high explosive bombs was mounted by way of reprisal. Ultimately some of the closely packed buildings were only captured when infantry broke through the walls on upper storeys with shaped charges. By the time Ortona was cleared, 1st Canadian Div had 2,339 casualties and was, at least temporarily, a spent force.

British analysis: 'Fighting in Built Up Areas' (1943)

From 1943 the British blueprint for urban combat in the Mediterranean theatre was *Fighting in Built Up Areas* – a manual that would be revised in 1945, and which later served as a template for much post-war literature. It both superseded and built upon the *Instructors' Handbook* that had been the main source of regular army tactical doctrine on the subject since October 1942.

Fighting in Built Up Areas stressed that urban warfare was not the work of specialists, but something with which all soldiers should be familiar. Nevertheless, built-up areas had special properties, not least of which was that they contained both very close, and very open, ground in close proximity – 'bordering every street are numerous protected firing positions, hiding places and sources of ambush. It follows that fighting will nearly always be at close quarters, casualties high, and the nerve strain for both sides heavy'. Restricted visibility meant an emphasis on short-range weapons, and two things were vital to the firefight: the importance of 'first shot' accuracy in making the most of the surprise encounter, and the absolute necessity of covering fire, even for the smallest operation.

The micro-tactics in both editions of *Fighting in Built Up Areas* were remarkably similar to those outlined for the Home Guard in January 1943. In capturing houses the teams acted as 'clearing' and 'covering' groups, working from the top of buildings downwards wherever possible.

Sub-machine guns, rifles and grenades were the staples of close action, while LMGs covered open areas and 'swamped' enemy covering fire. The little 2in platoon mortars were to be used for high explosive harrassing fire, or for smoke projection. Skilful operators were able to drop rounds into back gardens or other inaccessible spaces, or ricochet low-angle bombs off walls to land in nearby streets; the best mortarmen could even put an HE bomb through a chosen window. In March 1944 updated highlights of *Fighting in Built Up Areas* were included in the seminal *Infantry Training*. This emphasized the idea that 'fieldcraft', albeit of a very different sort, applied just as much to built-up areas as to the countryside.

Central to both *'FIBUA'* and *Infantry Training* was an established 'drill' for entire platoons involved in street clearance. This method assumed three rifle sections, plus a platoon HQ and reserve forming a fourth element. The first section and the HQ reserve were to deliver covering fire while the second and third sections took it in turns as the 'active' part of the operation, clearing one house at a time alternately up either side of a street. The employment of about three-quarters of the platoon weapons in covering fire at any given moment allowed the creation of particularly lethal 'killing zones', and a steady and systematic clearance with the least possiblity of 'friendly fire' casualties. This was unspectacular compared to some of the 'reconnaisance by fire' techniques employed by some combatants, but the methodical aproach was calculated to be sparing of troops and least prone to disaster. In villages, platoons were instructed to infiltrate an 'ambush party' around a flank wherever possible, to enfilade the most likely avenues of enemy retreat.

Cassino

The four battles fought around Monte Cassino, waged over a period of about five months during early 1944, involved Free French, British, Indian, US, Polish and New Zealand forces. While only part of the action took place in built-up areas, this aspect was extremely challenging, as explained by a US 34th Division report:

Enemy use of Cassino and its peculiar layout was extremely effective. The quadrangular arrangement of the houses around central courtyards, the irregular layout of the streets, and the heavy masonry of the buildings prevented our driving the enemy into the open to destroy him, and fields of fire for our weapons were very limited. The enemy was constantly aggressive and alert, and hand grenade fights were frequent, with grenades being thrown back and forth between buildings. The enemy employed his self-propelled guns audaciously, running them into the open to fire a few rounds and then withdrawing into cover ... among the buildings. Our tanks were hampered by narrow streets ... but on several occasions were

An improvised 'mouseholing charge' using two Hawkins (No.75) grenades, wooden staves, instantaneous primacord, safety fuse, tape and a detonator. The simultaneous explosion of a pair of these powerful bombs was enough to produce a hole big enough for a man to pass through most types of wall. The device, which was later refined to take four or five charges, has been reported as first used by 1st Canadian Div in Ortona, December 1943; but this illustration is from Home Guard Instruction No.51, *Patrolling*, of January 1943 – yet more evidence that Home Guard tactical training for urban warfare was among the most advanced in the Allied forces. (See also Elite 160, *World War II Infantry Assault Tactics*, Plate F.)

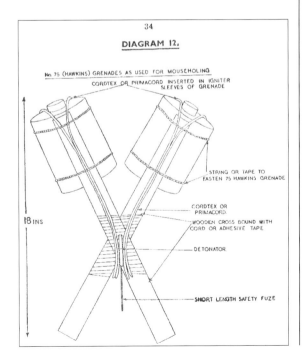

34

DIAGRAM 12.

No. 75 (HAWKINS) GRENADES AS USED FOR MOUSEHOLING

CORDTEX OR PRIMACORD INSERTED IN IGNITER SLEEVES OF GRENADE

STRING OR TAPE TO FASTEN 75 HAWKINS GRENADE

CORDTEX OR PRIMACORD.

WOODEN CROSS BOUND WITH CORD OR ADHESIVE TAPE

DETONATOR

18 INS

SHORT LENGTH SAFETY FUZE

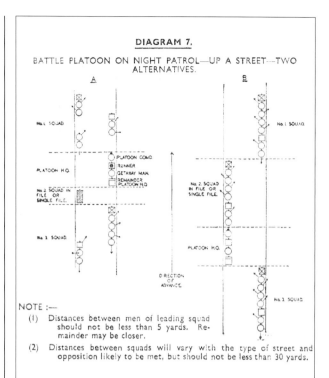

DIAGRAM 7.

BATTLE PLATOON ON NIGHT PATROL—UP A STREET—TWO ALTERNATIVES.

NOTE :—
(1) Distances between men of leading squad should not be less than 5 yards. Remainder may be closer.
(2) Distances between squads will vary with the type of street and opposition likely to be met, but should not be less than 30 yards.

Two alternative formations for a platoon advancing up a street, from the Home Guard manual *Patrolling* (January 1943). In 'A' the leading section is divided between both sides of the street, followed by platoon HQ on one side, followed by the complete second section on the other side, and finally by the third section divided between both sides. In 'B' each complete section takes alernate sides of the street, with HQ following the second section.

able to destroy enemy strongpoints in buildings with point blank fire. During the entire occupation of Cassino by our troops, the enemy-held portions of the town were subjected to extremely heavy artillery concentrations, including 8 inch and 240mm fire, but his attitude remained unchanged.

By the time of the New Zealand and Indian assault during the third battle in mid February, bombardment by waves of bombers and entire regiments of artillery – followed by rain – had reduced the buildings of Cassino to what one report described as the consistency of dough. Colonel Nangle and his Gurkhas encountered 'an unbelievable mess' with no vestige of road or track, 'only vast heaps of rubble out of which peered the jagged edges of walls'. Yet weight of munitions proved insufficient to crush the German resistance, which hinged on concrete pillboxes, and on cellars converted into reinforced dugouts by means of a sandwich of beams, earth, and spaces designed to absorb blast. At the Continental Hotel a Panzer was built into the wreckage. As the New Zealanders worked their way into the town the use of heavy weapons became increasingly difficult, until the positions of defenders and attackers became throughly intermingled. In one famous instance a platoon survived for 36 hours inside a house upon whose roof Germans could be heard moving about. Covering fire from other strongpoints and grenades dropped from above prevented the attackers from either moving away, or dislodging their adversaries.

Experiences like this during Operation 'Dickens' led Allied Force Headquarters to issue *Training Memorandum No.5* – an attempt to co-ordinate and rationalize the efforts of ground and air forces in urban operations. Where sufficient tactical aircaft were available it was advised that strategic bombers were best omitted from the order of battle. Where they had to be used, they would make their runs parallel to the front so that 'shorts' would not fall on friendly troops, and delay fuses would allow cellars to be penetrated before the bombs exploded. Tonnage was to be carefully regulated, and the attack following any sort of bombardment must be 'immediate and aggressive, employing the maximum of infantry strength'. Mortars and tank-destroyers were to be moved up quickly, being suitable for immediate support of ground operations. Where an enemy-occupied built-up area had to be traversed it was desirable for armour to attempt to move through in a quick thrust, with the objective of preventing the enemy bringing up reinforcements and supplies which might turn a skirmish into a major battle of attrition. These were all useful lessons; but *Training Memorandum No.5* was not promulgated until 14 June 1944, and it is doubtful whether all it contained had been throughly absorbed until well after D-Day.

'Mouseholing': during the American operations in Brest, troops blast their way into a building through a thick exterior wall of dressed stone. In the first picture a large charge (apparently of 12x ½lb blocks) is placed carefully in a ground-level basement window – incidentally, exactly the type of position favoured for heavy weapons during the defence of city blocks. The team must have stood well back under cover during the explosion of 6lb of TNT; in the second photo a GI crawls inside the building through the hole torn by the blast. (IWM HU 94979 & 94980)

THE US ARMY IN NW EUROPE

Doctrine: *FM 31-50*

By late 1943 combat experience and the analysis of enemy methods had led to the development of street-fighting tactics that would see US forces through to the end of the war. This doctrine, which superseded the existing *Training Circulars 33* and *41*, as well as basic advice offered in the 1941 manuals, was published in January 1944 as the remarkable Field Manual 31-50, *Attack on a Fortified Position and Combat in Towns*. This was the key document from which GIs were taught street fighting prior to the invasion of France in June 1944.

As was already commonly accepted, FM 31-50 first recommended that street fighting was still best avoided if at all possible. If it was inescapable,

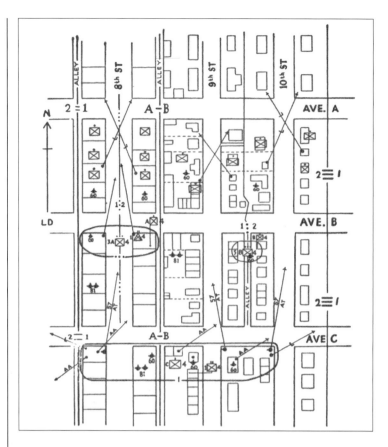

then US troops were encouraged to consider six basic factors:

(1) Cover and concealment are available to both sides.

(2) Streets and alleys invite movement, but constitute lanes readily swept by fire.

(3) Observation and fields of fire are limited.

(4) Operation of mechanized vehicles is ordinarily greatly restricted and canalized, subjecting them to close-range attack by various weapons. Tanks are at a further disadvantage because of inability to elevate or depress their main weapons to fire into the upper floors or basements of nearby buildings.

(5) Close proximity of opposing forces will ordinarily limit the effectiveness of close support by artillery and aircraft.

(6) Communications will be impeded, thus making the decentralization of control to small units imperative. This necessarily entails a high degree of initiative and a thorough understanding of the situation by junior leaders.

Textbook US plan for the taking of a built-up area, from FM 31-50, *Attack on a Fortified Position and Combat in Towns* (January 1944). Individual platoon lines of advance are plotted, moving northwards up the diagram. For command purposes the area is divided up horizontally by Avenues A, B and C, and by imaginary vertical lines up the map. In this instance no block-by-block action is required. The expectation was that the geometric grid layout of towns would help the attackers keep a sense of direction; in practice this would not often work, since most old European towns had less rational street-plans that had developed 'organically' over the centuries.

As to the built-up environment itself, it was suggested that this could be divided into three types. Outskirts were characterized by isolated houses, or groups of houses, surrounded by gardens, trees, fields and vacant lots. When isolated, a house was perhaps best considered as an 'inferior pillbox'. Semi-detached property and other close housing was regarded as an 'intermediate stage'; while town centres were usually built in blocks, with little space between, but often with cellars and basements rendering defence much more effective. As the manual rather euphemistically explained, all types of townscape were likely to be 'modified' by combat, the resulting heaps of rubble being 'analogous to close country providing much cover' and restricting movement.

Troops were to be aware that built-up areas possessed a 'third dimension', as an enemy could be bypassed by going under or over, and it was usually the case that the combatant on top had the advantage over the one below. Dust and noise were also magnified in towns, and both these factors could be turned to advantage, as for example when the noise from a sniper's rifle bounced from many surfaces, giving a misleading impression of his distance and direction. Manoeuvre was restricted, as was observation – so much so that towns were often comparable to 'dense jungle' in terms of control problems.

According to US doctrine, neutralization of hostile fire was of paramount importance. As opposing forces were likely to be close, the

(continued on page 41)

STREET-FIGHTERS
1: British Home Guard sniper, 1942
2: Gurt Bn, Polish Home Army; Warsaw, August 1944
3: Flamethrower operator, 3rd Canadian Div; Normandy, June 1944

A

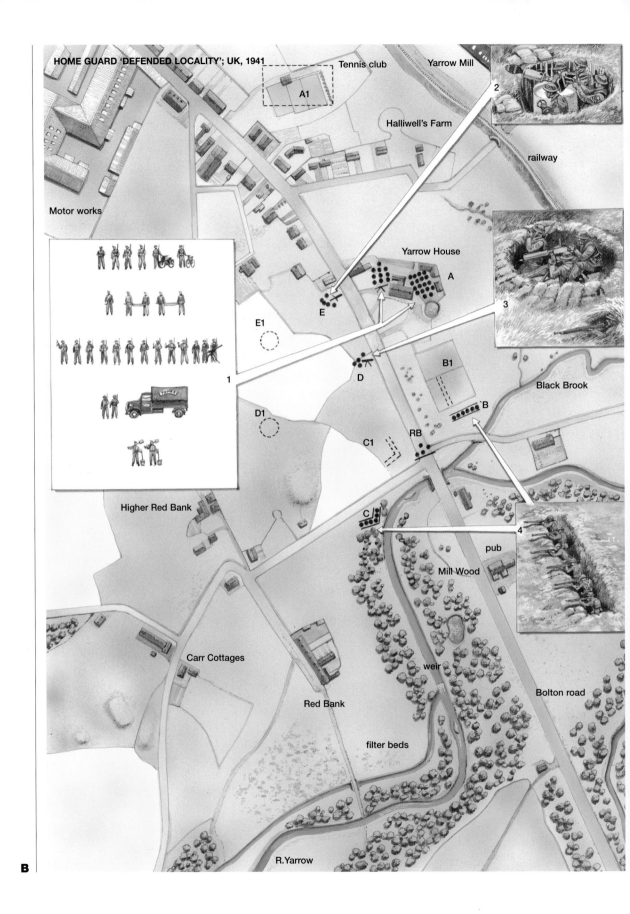

HOME GUARD 'DEFENDED LOCALITY'; UK, 1941

Tennis club

A1

Yarrow Mill

Yarrow House

Halliwell's Farm

railway

Motor works

A

E

E1

Yarrow House

B1

Black Brook

D

D1

C1

RB

`B

Higher Red Bank

C

pub

Mill Wood

Carr Cottages

weir

Bolton road

Red Bank

filter beds

R.Yarrow

1

2

3

4

B

RED ARMY 'STORM GROUP'; STALINGRAD 1942

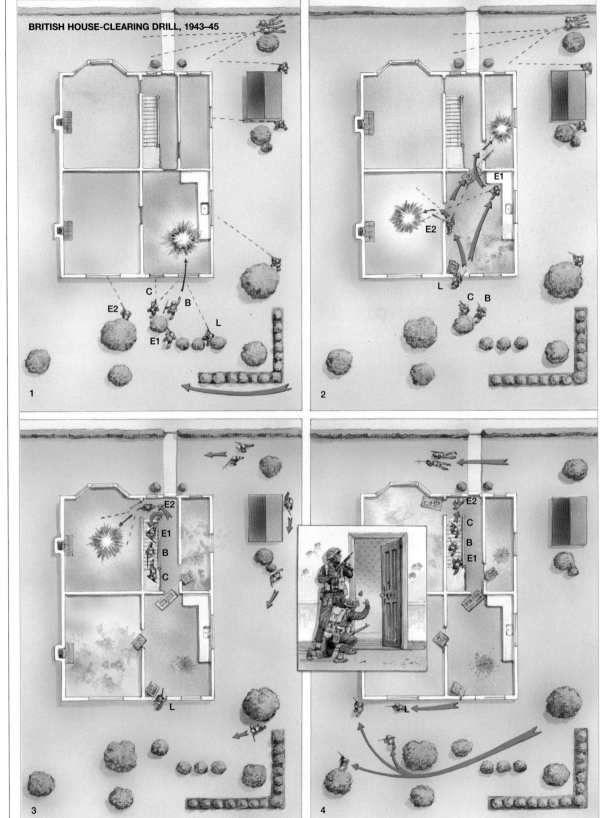

BRITISH HOUSE-CLEARING DRILL, 1943–45

BARYKADY FIGHTING; WARSAW, AUGUST 1944

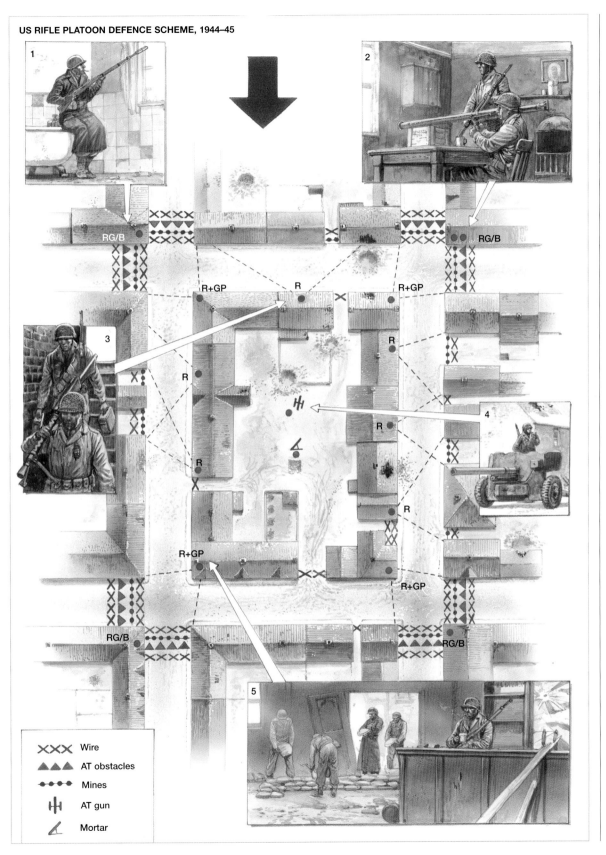

US RIFLE PLATOON DEFENCE SCHEME, 1944–45

1

2

3

RG/B

RG/B

R+GP

R

R+GP

R

R

R

R

R

R

R

4

R+GP

R+GP

RG/B

RG/B

5

✕✕✕ Wire

▲▲▲ AT obstacles

•••• Mines

╫ AT gun

⊿ Mortar

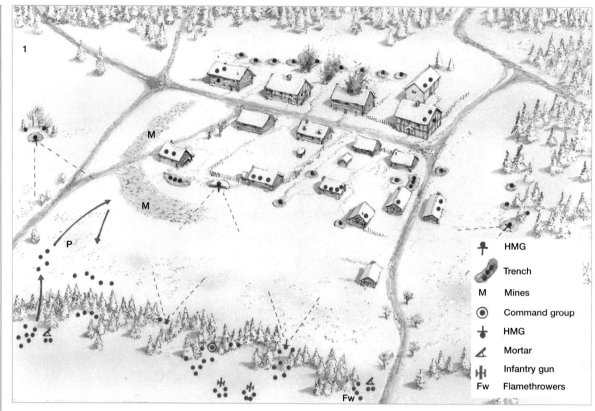

GERMAN ATTACK ON SOVIET-HELD VILLAGE, 1944–45

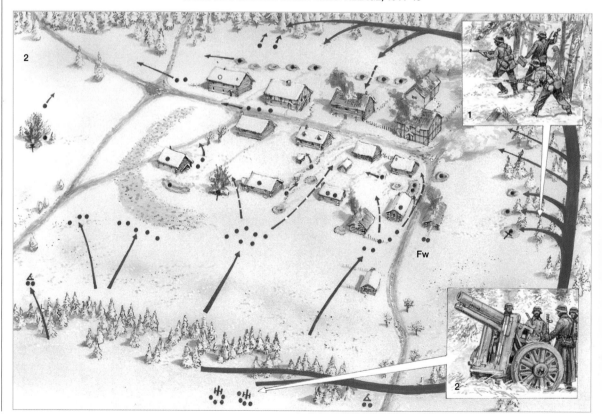

regimental anti-tank company and infantry
cannon company would play a critical part;
moreover, the bulk of the mortars and
machine guns must be well forward –
'covering fire is essential for every operation,
and must be provided with the smallest unit
in addition to that furnished by larger units'.
Smoke was important, particularly for small
units, to blind enemy observation and for
deception and surprise. Much of the actual
combat would occur at night when streets
could be crossed more safely, and infiltration
and combat with hostile patrols might ensue.

Ruthlessness was often required, as
'frequently the quickest, surest, and most
economical way of dislodging an enemy from
a building will be to burn it'. Spies and fifth-columnists 'must be
ceaselessly sought out and mercilessly dealt with'. Interestingly, while
much of the passage regarding civilians was identical to the 1943 British
manual *Fighting in Built Up Areas*, this was one of the few important
differences. British policy recommended that in 'friendly towns'
evacuation might be best, or if it were not achievable then women and
children could be moved to certain sectors. When an enemy area was
taken, 'non essential' civilians were to be evacuated from important
parts as quickly as possible, and any allowed to remain could be given a
coloured pass. In this way spies or hostile civilians could be strictly
excluded. It might not always have worked, but the clear implication is
that the preferred British method was to get civilians safely out of the
way first, rather than get involved in the difficult business of sifting out
for 'merciless' treatment those deemed suspect.

For the attack, the US manual advised two phases. The first was the
capture of 'an initial position within the built up area, the possession of
which will eliminate hostile fields of fire, reduce the effectiveness of
hostile long range flat trajectory fires, and limit enemy observation'.
With this achieved, phase two became possible – an advance through the
built-up area. To succeed in this, provision had to be made to
decentralize control, and later to regain control of subordinate units; to
organize 'mopping up'; and to maintain communication between the
artillery and infantry. Usually it would also be desirable to secure
supporting positions outside the built-up area. Supply would also
require careful attention, since roads were likely to be blocked; every
effort must be used to push supplies as far forward as practical under
cover, with carrying-parties made available as soon as mechanical means
became impossible. Large stocks of grenades and explosives were
needed for house-to-house fighting and demolition.

Regimental organization for the attack assigned relatively narrow
battalion frontages, tailored so as to fit the types of buildings and
defence involved. A high proportion of the support weapons would be
attached to the attacking sub-units. Engineers would play their part by
clearing mines, barriers and booby traps, carrying out demolitions and
making temporary repairs. Battalion dispositions would be altered
according to circumstance, but the usual procedure was to allot each

Aachen, October 1944:
a US 57mm AT gun has been
positioned, partly protected by a
bank of rubble and camouflaged
with debris, to fire down a street.
Deployed in this way, artillery and
machine guns could create 'killing
grounds' that were extremely
dangerous to cross. Even
obsolescent AT weapons like
the US and German 3.7cm guns
were useful in street fighting;
they were fairly easy to
manhandle and to conceal in
rubble and ruins, and could
give effective supporting fire
to attacking infantry.
(US Signal Corps)

company to one or at most two city blocks. Defined areas were established by the battalion commander, and the attack was regulated one block at a time, with successive objectives – for example, reaching a rail line, or capturing a particular street. A number of AT and supporting artillery weapons might be attached for the reduction of specific targets. A 'battalion reserve' held back a few blocks away was handy to protect flanks, envelop the enemy, or mop up.

Individual platoons would not be concerned with more than one block at a time, the conduct of a block-by-block assault requiring 'alert, aggressive leadership on the part of the platoon leader'. He was to make full use of supporting machine guns, and to regard 60mm mortars as 'weapons of opportunity' for use against snipers or enemy without overhead cover, since their bombs would make relatively little impression on large buildings. The 81mm mortar could be used as a building-buster, however, since its bomb would wreck a light structure and could penetrate the roof of many others. Platoon commanders were not to be shy in requesting assault guns or other heavy weapons for the reduction of particularly difficult buildings. When a frontal attack was necessary the platoon commander was to be sure to organize plenty of smoke, or the shooting of incendiary ammunition against barricades and other obstructions.

Whatever tanks and tank-destroyers were available required careful handling, and were best attached in small numbers to perform such jobs as meeting hostile counter-attacks, or singly to smash specific buildings or overcome barricades; flamethrower tanks could neutralize strongpoints or drive the enemy from cover. All tanks had to have close infantry support. Artillery would necessarily be reliant on forward observers, light howitzers being best for lobbing shells into built-up areas.

At the lowest level, rifle squads could be employed as 'assault squads' with special equipment and personnel attached as required. These squads varied according to the task, but were essentially the same as those employed in attacks on fortifications. One of the best models was to take a rifle company and an engineer platoon, and from their

GIs doing some rather sloppy house clearance in the streets of Metz. According to the established drill the BAR team (left) should be hanging well back, covering likely exits and the rest of the team as they break into the house. US training specifically warned against the kind of 'bunching' of the squad seen here. (IWM EA 44646)

resources organize a couple of assault units – perhaps with a bazooka team and an LMG team attached. The remainder of the company would be employed in 'support'. An example of a typical 12-man assault squad was given:

Squad leader, with rifle, grenades and signalling equipment.

Two-man 'demolition party', with rifles, demolition charges and grenades.

Flamethrower operator, with flamethrower, grenades and pistol.

'Rocketeer', with bazooka, rocket, grenades and pistol.

Assistant 'rocketeer', with rockets, rifle, and grenades.

Wire-cutting party:

Assistant squad leader, with rifle, wire cutters, [rifle] grenade launcher, grenades and signalling equipment.

Automatic rifleman, with BAR and grenades.

Assistant automatic rifleman, with rifle, grenade-launcher and grenades.

Three riflemen, with rifles, bangalore torpedoes, wire cutters, grenades and grenade-launcher.

Naturally, where there was little or no barbed wire other special equipment could be substituted. Possible options might include beehive charges, satchel charges and/or pole charges; incendiaries; carbines; and sledgehammers and axes.[5]

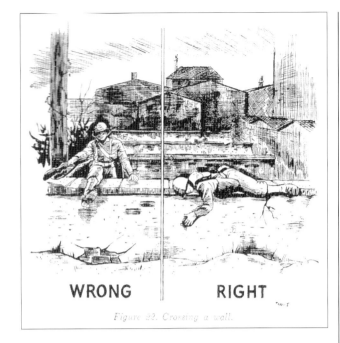

WRONG   RIGHT

Figure 22. Crossing a wall.

FM 31-50 did not forget such obvious advice as the right way to cross a wall, avoiding making a conspicuous break in its profile by slithering over quickly and dropping down on the other side, to scurry away or adopt a prone firing position.

House-to-house fighting

Any riflemen involved in general house-to-house fighting were warned against carrying too much equipment; helmets, rifles, bayonets and grenades were regarded as the irreducible minimum, but certain items were particularly useful if available. These included SMGs (not standard issue to the US rifle platoon), pistols, knives, toggle ropes and grappling hooks. All infantry units involved in street fighting were to make sure that they had some crowbars and axes for breaking through doors, walls and roofs. If rubber-soled footwear was provided it should be worn, but socks or burlap strips could also be used to deaden the noise of boots during covert work.

Whether a special 'assault squad' or not, every group of men was to have a clear and specific task as a 'covering party' or a 'search party'. Search parties were to enter enemy-held buildings; given the limited space, they should be kept small and operate to pre-prepared plans. Typically such parties might consist of a squad leader with four to six riflemen. Just one or two of the team would make the first move, under cover of the others, and force an entry into a building. The remainder followed quickly, posting themselves so as to prevent surprise.

Three house-clearing methods were recommended: coming in through the roof and working systematically downward to the cellar;

[5] See Elite 160, *World War II Infantry Assault Tactics*, for more detailed material on the role and equipment of combat engineers in the assault.

Men of the US 331st Infantry, 83rd 'Ohio' Inf Div come under sniper fire during the advance through St Malo, France. The squad have been advancing down the right-hand side of the street, and now attempt to return fire while still hugging the walls – tricky, for right-handed shots, and one soldier doubles across the street in search of a better firing position. Note the .30cal machine-gunner (far right), with a fighting knife strapped low on his leg. (IWM EA 32725)

entry on the ground floor by means of explosives; or entry through doors and windows. The first option was the best, since the enemy might then decide to evacuate the building – and be caught by the fire of covering parties as he did so. Cornered enemy troops might well 'fight desperately', so making it appear that there was an escape route for them was a useful trick. Fighting downwards also worked with gravity, since grenades could be dropped or thrown downstairs or through holes. If the enemy proved stubborn in wooden-floored structures, another ruse was to prepare a mattress, pull the pins from a couple of grenades on the floor, drop the mattress over the bombs, and throw oneself clear. The downward blast might cause distraction below while other friendly troops came into action, or at the very least would unleash clouds of dust to temporarily unsight the enemy.

When entering buildings from ground level the best method was to get upstairs as quickly as possible; if this really could not be achieved then downstairs rooms would have to be taken first, with periodic sprays of bullets up through the ceiling to keep any enemy upstairs occupied. Where it was believed the enemy occupied a room, tossing in a grenade – preferably through something other than the main entrance – was the preferred option:

The attackers must work in pairs, using the 'buddy' system, with each man alternately covering his buddy's movements. In this system, one man throws the grenade into the room. The other rushes immediately after the explosion, stands with his back to the wall and his rifle ready for instantaneous use, and covers his partner as he searches the room for occupants. In entering rooms through doorways, riflemen should crouch as low as possible and jump to one side of the door. The defender usually will have his point of aim at approximately waist height. In breaching a wall, take precautions for protection from enemy fire through the wall and keep the hole covered by fire to prevent him throwing the first grenade. Before throwing grenades at windows or doorways, look to see they are not covered. Do not assume that a grenade bursting in a room has disabled all of the enemy. In a defended room, the enemy may erect a barricade in a corner as protection from grenades. Watch out for such a barricade and have another grenade ready to throw behind it.

Key tactical considerations in taking streets included choice of cover, and the strict avoidance of bunching. Leaving any enemy-occupied house in the rear was 'fatal'. Streets were to be crossed only quickly and with caution, since it was 'suicidal to delay in the open'. Troops were to hug walls as they moved, firing around rather than over cover, altering from right- to left-handed shooting to match the layout of buildings. Rooftops and walls were better rolled over than stood on, as moving stiffly upright attracted attention and created recognizable silhouettes. Automatic squad weapons were best deployed to fire down streets or to cover open ground. Wariness of booby traps was critical, although if the enemy currently occupied a building himself, the likelihood of encountering traps was reduced.

As good as FM 31-50 was, and however well it translated best German practice for use by the American soldier, there was no panacea that could take away the extreme danger of urban combat. Nor was there sufficient training to ensure that every infantryman succeeded in absorbing all of its lessons. There were also modifications and additions to the basic system, most notably in the ever-closer integration of infantry and armour.

A US infantry/armour team during the fighting for Aachen. The nearest tank – piled with a variety of equipment, including for some reason a BAR-man's web gear – is a 'dozer' Sherman, valuable for pushing aside roadblocks and rubble. Note the prone rifleman, using the blade as cover while attempting to engage snipers. The massive masonry of the wall is a reminder of the sheer strength of the defended buildings often faced during city-centre fighting. (IWM HU 94981)

Tank/infantry co-operation

In the 2nd 'Hell on Wheels' Armd Div, for example, it became standard practice for infantry and tanks to support each other against occupied villages by fire and movement; then, in a carefully choreographed sequence, the target would be struck by artillery and combat air support; finally, one tank platoon provided fire support while another tank-and-infantry team advanced into the village from another angle, so that the fire of the supporting armour was not obscured.

On first entering the village the mixed team would begin with 'reconnaissance by fire', spraying suspected enemy positions. If resistance was thus subdued, the support armour could be moved up, and finally through the village to positions where it was ready to meet any counter-attack. If resistance was not suppressed, the support force could manoeuvre around the village to fire on the enemy from unexpected angles, assisting the assault forward a building or two at a time.

The tank battalion manual FM 17-33 went so far as to recommend that an ideal opening to an attack on a built-up area was to encircle it by

Neuss, Germany: a US Sherman tank in close support of men of the 83rd Inf Div – from the dozens of discarded shell packing tubes, it is being completely re-stocked with ammunition after prolonged firing. In the close-range house-busting role tanks were valuable, but always in peril from the hand-held AT weapons of German tank-hunter teams stalking them through the ruins. Here a veritable sandbag wall, suspended on logs and stake-and-wire frames, has been built up around the hull in the hope of detonating Panzerfaust and Panzershreck projectiles before they reach the armour.

means of an armoured thrust. Smaller numbers of tanks might then be committed to support actual street fighting, firing HE rounds 'against street barricades and houses containing snipers. Steeples, tall chimneys and other structures likely to contain artillery observers are promptly destroyed.' Tank crews were not to halt or drive slowly near buildings which had not been occupied by friendly infantry, and were to be alert to the possibilty of disguised pillboxes built into street-front properties.

The *Operations* manual FM 100-5 of June 1944 offered another useful alternative, in which enemy town garrisons were fixed by a holding attack only, while the 'main' attack was used to isolate the enemy from relief. If the town did not then capitulate, it would be attacked with the main force, but a mechanized reserve would be held back to intervene against any counter-attacks. This would provide an effective antidote in instances where the German town commander was himself using 'sword and shield tactics', with a defensive and an offensive element to his strategy.

Raids were similarly turned to good account, and were often conducted at night with the objective of damaging enemy morale and inflicting casualties while discovering how well any town or village might be defended. The African-American 614th Tank Destroyer Bn was one unit which excelled in this role; with tongue in cheek, they referred to their terrifying night-time exploits as 'minstrel shows'. What was later hailed as 'the perfect raid' was mounted by Sgt D.H. Forrester and seven men of 103rd Recon Troop at Rothbach. This surprise probe lasted just 17 minutes, but was launched under cover of a 276-round diversionary artillery barrage. Reaching the house selected as the main target, Forrester left four men as a covering party, bursting into the house with the others in textbook manner. He sprayed the first room with his SMG, disabling four enemy and taking a fifth prisoner. At this, ten other Germans spilled out into the snow from other exits, only to be cut down by the guns of the covering party. By the time the raiders regained their own lines they had claimed 18 enemy casualties and a prisoner, against just one man of their own slightly wounded.

Practical experience

Urban actions could just as easily go badly awry, however. At Brest – many GIs' baptism of fire in street fighting – the Germans were well prepared, both in the town centre and in a network of pillboxes and emplacements to the north. For ten days the Americans battled through the streets, fighting a 'corporal's war' in which a company was often required to take a single block. The US 23rd Inf Regt of the 2nd 'Indianhead' Inf Div was faced by the town cemetery, which was covered by interlocking zones of fire from surrounding buildings and MGs emplaced in burial vaults, and head-on attacks were halted in a hail of bullets and marble chippings. This impasse was only resolved when the regiment worked its way around the burial ground, 'mouseholing' from house to house, while tank-destroyers were brought up to fire at point blank range.

At Aachen in October 1944, First US Army attacked the first German city reached by the Western Allies with overwhelming strength. As LtCol Daniel of the 26th Infantry reported: 'The general plan evolved was to use artillery and mortar fire across our front to isolate the sector... then to use direct fire from tanks, tank destroyers, and machine guns to pin down the defenders and chase them into cellars; and then to move in with bayonets and hand grenades.' But the German defenders from 246.Volksgrenadier Div were under strict orders to hold out to the last man, and the attackers were forced to break down their units into combined-arms teams and clear the streets building by building. Each rifle company of the 2/26th was allocated three tanks or tank-destroyers, two towed AT guns, two extra bazookas, two HMGs and a flamethrower team. Artillery batteries fired with delay fuses, which allowed the shells to penetrate down through buildings before exploding for maximum destruction. Self-propelled 155mm guns were brought up to fire directly into strongpoints. While liberal applications of firepower were ordered, US commanders also deviated from the manual by ordering the evacuation of all civilians. For the actual infantry attack each small assault team was covered by a tank:

> These would keep each building under fire until the riflemen moved in to assault; thereupon the armour would shift fire to the next house. Augmented by the battalion's light and heavy machine guns firing up the streets, this shelling drove the Germans into the cellars, where the infantry stormed them behind a barrage of hand grenades. Whenever the enemy proved particularly tenacious, the riflemen used other weapons ... including demolitions and flamethrowers employed by two-man teams attached to each company headquarters. The men did not wait for actual targets to appear; each building they assumed was a nest of resistance until proved otherwise. Light artillery and mortar fire swept forward block by block several streets ahead of the infantry, while heavier artillery pounded German communications further to the rear.

Despite these tactics, US casualties amounted to about 500 men – not many by Eastern Front standards, but a real shock to those unaccustomed to intensive street fighting. Key problems proved to be 'stay-behind' squads –

Venlo, Netherlands, December 1944: lightly equipped British troops – they have dropped their packs – cautiously flush out enemy snipers from the suburb of Blerick. The taking of Blerick involved the bridging of an anti-tank ditch at five points while under fire, but by 5 December all German resistance was reduced to small groups. Once located, isolated snipers could be dealt with by returning fire from one direction while clearing parties worked their way around from another.

who held their fire only to emerge from cellars and storm-drains to engage the Americans from the rear – and snipers. Some of these latter, when captured, turned out to be Hitler Youth and children as young as ten.

Around Schillersdorf in Alsace early in 1945, the 103rd 'Cactus' Div discovered just how confused urban fighting could be. Before reaching the village they were subjected to 'jitter' tactics, with shouted insults in the night and enemy troops lurking in the snow apparently wearing US uniforms; an enemy counter-attack against 410th Inf Regt then ejected the Americans from the village. This was due at least in part to the freezing-up of a machine gun which had been the key weapon covering the crossroads. A few men attempted to work their way behind the Germans, not realizing that they were being attacked by a battalion. Texan Pfc M.L. Jacobs shot one German, then attempted to run away through a courtyard, only to find that as he opened the door an enemy soldier was already pulling on the handle the other side. Running back again, Jacobs was then forced to hide under a wagon. Later he managed to hide, with two others, in the attic of a barn, where they stayed for two days. The remaining defenders made their escape as best they could; the next day two US battalions retook the village, supported by tanks and artillery.

GERMANY, 1945

German forces

The final summation of German town- and street-fighting methods appeared as sections in the US War Department manual *Handbook on German Military Forces* (March 1945); this gave a good idea of the techniques which Allied forces faced once they had breached the frontiers of the Reich. Many aspects were familiar – including the formation of main lines of resistance well within built-up areas rather than on vulnerable peripheries. Also deemed of enduring value were strongpoints beyond this MLR, intended to break up Allied attacks; mobile counter-attack forces held in readiness both inside and outside a town (though by now the Wehrmacht was badly under strength for such luxuries); and the use of flanking weapons which held their fire until presented with good targets. However, the methods recommended at the beginning of 1945 were far more comprehensive than the outlines thought sufficient at the start of the war.

In village strongpoints it was now usual to have a designated Kampfkommandant or battle commander, whose writ as senior officer and tactical leader extended to all military forces, emergency units and civil organizations in the locality, and who ranked as a regimental commander for disciplinary purposes. The appointment of Kampfkommandanten was intended to simplify the overlapping purviews of the Wehrmacht, SS, Party organizations, air-raid services and any *ad hoc* formations, making for tactical fluency in the defensive battle.

In small villages it was usually sufficient to consolidate on the settlement, but for larger villages and towns a series of concentric positions might allow defenders to fall back gradually in the face of overwhelming force. Within the built-up area itself this might include a perimeter, intermediate positions, and a final inner ring. The perimeter defence commonly consisted of 'one or more continuous trench systems, each with a deep main battle zone', and this perimeter would often extend beyond the outskirts of the village. Artillery and other heavy support weapons were deployed so as to support these field works, perhaps with single guns

detached and placed to defend strongpoints or cover roads. Outside a significant built-up area there might be further concentric defence lines, as far as 4 to 6 miles out, thus forcing Allied artillery to displace repeatedly to engage them one at a time. For a major town or city the outermost defence line might be as far as 18 miles from the outskirts, with further advanced positions another mile out.

Patrols would be mounted to warn of enemy approach and to mount ambushes. The boundaries of unit sectors were not coincidental with main roads, to avoid any possibility of these being neglected accidentally; significant approach routes fell within the definite jurisdiction of a battalion or company.

Tanks were not thought particularly useful to a defending force within a town, but were used 'in static dug-in positions at cross-roads

Cologne, Germany, March 1945: these US troops are relaxed enough to advance at an easy walk down the bomb-shattered streets. However, most of the platoon still spread out to either side of the road, and a watch is maintained from the doorway in the foreground.

Kervenheim, Germany, March 1945: men of the 2nd Bn Royal Norfolks, 3rd Inf Div, demonstrate the correct way to cross a street in battle: swiftly, and well spread out. This frame catches three members of a squad at the run, only one of whom is actually fully exposed in the road.

'Platoon Battle Drill for Clearing Two Rows of Occupied Houses', from the British manual *Fighting in Built Up Areas* (1943, reprinted with amendments 1945). The objective is 'Street or Back Area B' at the centre – i.e. the drill applied equally to clearing the terraced houses by access from the street in front, or from the row of yards or gardens behind them. Throughout, cordons of fire down Streets A, B and C are provided by the Bren gun and rifles of No.1 Section (Z), supported by the 2in mortar and PIAT of Platoon HQ. Street B is systematically cleared by Nos.2 and 3 Sections (X & Y). Each clearing party is initially covered by fire from its section LMG team; as each house is cleared, the LMG team follow the clearing party into it, and cover the next facing house; the other section are then signalled that the LMG is in place, and clear the facing house; and so the clearing parties and LMGs move methodically up the street, covering one another. The platoon HQ follows up gradually, keeping a small reserve in hand for emergencies. Sometimes a fire element might be sent around a flank to establish a blocking ambush at the far end to catch retreating enemy.

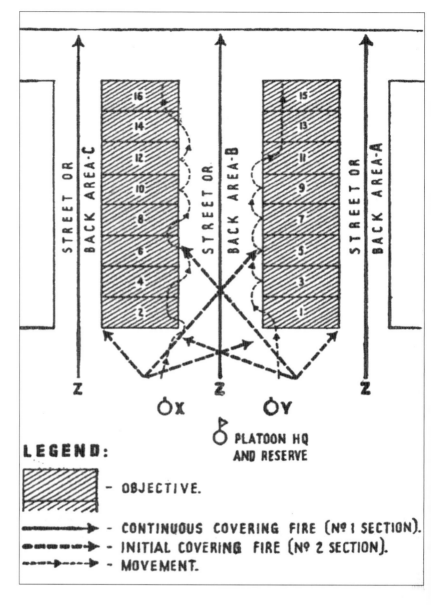

and squares'. Assault guns and tanks were also placed inside buildings, and could support counter-attacks; in such situations infantry would be assigned to their close protection. German hand-held AT weapons were commonly used from foxholes outside the perimeter of a town; where they were used within the built-up area, they were best fired from pits, behind hedges or round walls, especially from flanking positions. Neither the Panzerfaust nor the Panzerschreck were suitable for use in enclosed spaces, due to their powerful *Feuerstrahl* or back-blast.[6] Efforts were also made to destroy immobilized Allied AFVs, inside or outside a town, to prevent their recovery.

Individual buildings required individual treatments, but some measures were universal:

---

6 See Elite 124, *World War II Infantry Anti-Tank Tactics*

Both occupied and unoccupied buildings are booby trapped… Entrances to buildings are blocked, and all windows opened so as not to disclose those from which fire is maintained. Rooms are darkened, and passages are cut in the walls between buildings. To avoid detection, the Germans fire from the middle of the rooms, and frequently change their positions, while communication is maintained through cellars and over roofs. Machine guns are sited low, usually in basements, to provide better grazing fire. Chimneys and cornices are used as cover for men on roofs; tiles may be removed to provide loopholes. Searchlights are mounted to illuminate fields of fire; in their absence vehicle headlights may be used as substitutes. When houses collapse, the defense is carried on from cellars, and rubble-heaps of destroyed areas are organized into strong points.

As had long since been established, German forces attacking through built-up areas were usually deployed as a number of columns whose task was to advance parallel to each other along suitable axes, dividing up the town into smaller pockets. These columns were themselves divided into 'assault' and 'mopping-up' groups. In the hands of the assault groups were concentrated engineer resources such as demolition equipment and flamethrowers. Where possible the advance would not be along streets but through gardens and holes blasted in walls, preferably covered by other troops from tall buildings.

When compelled to advance through streets, the Germans move in two files, one on each side… The left side is preferred as it is more advantageous for firing right-handed from doorways. Consideration is given to the problem of fighting against defenders organized not only in depth but in height. Consequently the men receive specific assignments to watch the rooms, the various floors of buildings, and cellar windows. Side streets are immediately blocked, and at night searchlights are kept ready to illuminate roofs. As soon as a building is occupied, the Germans organize it into a strongpoint. Windows and other openings are converted into loopholes and embrasures. Cellars and attics are occupied first [when] organizing for defence.

Well-known photo of British Airborne personnel occupying a modified shellhole in a partially built-up suburban area during the Arnhem fighting. Paratroop companies were well suited for urban fighting, having a higher than usual complement of automatic weapons. A typical nine-man section included a section sergeant as well as at least one corporal or lance-corporal; its weapons were two Sten guns (though the corporal in this group prefers the longer effective range of a rifle), a Bren, six rifles – one in the hands of the section sniper – and an assortment of grenades including anti-tank 'Gammon bombs'.

Baal, Germany, February 1945: a 4.2in heavy mortar of a US Chemical Mortar Battalion, caught at the moment of discharge at a shallow angle, while supporting the infantry clearing the town. Boards and a heap of sandbags are used to prevent the heavy recoil from moving the weapon or driving the baseplate into the soft ground. Although originally intended primarily for the delivery of smoke – thus the designation of the units equipped with it – the 4.2in packed a heavy high-trajectory punch that was useful in built-up areas. (US Signal Corps)

Allied forces

Excellent as German methods undoubtedly were, the balance of power in urban fighting had shifted inexorably in favour of the Allies from 1943 onwards. Weight of numbers, artillery and air support were used to great advantage – but equally importantly, Allied infantry had now learned sophisticated tactics to overcome intelligent urban defence. Some of these involved the movements of battalions, some the drills of squads, but the conduct of the individual soldier instructed in urban 'battlecraft' was recognized as the starting point for success.

In 1945 the British manual *Fighting in Built Up Areas* offered a list of 15 simple 'do's and don'ts'. Thinking ahead and 'reading' buildings were vital skills. Junior leaders were to make mental preparations for emergencies, considering different structures from the point of view of the enemy, and imagining which parts they would be likely to occupy. They were also to use common sense in adopting positions in buildings, for example not placing firers and observers close together in the same room, where the noise of firing would deaden perception and prevent the observer from 'watching with his ears'. Similarly, 'jabbering' in action was to be avoided: the correct command at the right moment was vital, but too much shouting disconcerted friends and gave too much information to the enemy. The physical environment, smoke and dust were all to be used to advantage, and not allowed to hinder; smoke was to be used lavishly rather than sparingly, since thin screens were almost useless. In domestic interiors, tables, mattresses and other items could be made useful, while removing plaster and damping the ground would prevent tell-tale clouds of choking dust; the soldier must overcome his natural 'disinclination to wreck a place', using anything and everything to defeat the enemy.

As far as movement was concerned, frequent changes of position were desirable, preferably by crawling or 'worming' and always keeping as low as possible. In adopting firing or observation positions it was vital to move slowly, since rapid movements attracted attention. Walls or crests were best slithered over, face downwards, keeping the body as horizontal as possible. When crossing a street or climbing stairs any distraction, such as throwing something, might buy an extra fraction of a second. Corners were to be looked around at ground level.

When shooting in an urban setting, the most skilled men held their fire 'until the psychological moment', and entrapped the opposition rather than merely driving them off. When firing at loopholes accuracy was vital, one deliberate shot or burst being better than two or three hurried ones. Exceptions to this general rule were when 'browning' the enemy through a wall, floor or ceiling, or when taking a quick snap-shot on the move.

Flamethrowers

Aggressive flamethrower tactics – once an area of virtually undisputed German mastery – were now a key component of Allied urban warfare tactics. By 1944, US portable flamethrowers were being used with both 'thin' and new 'thickened' fuels (such as napalm); the latter increased effective range and caused the blazing fuel to cling, both to embrasures and targets. Operators learned to approach the objective obliquely, using cover to conceal their bulky tanks, and to take advantage of the fact that the liquid spread when it hit and could 'turn corners', pouring through openings from which the defenders could not return fire. A gout of flame was often a good last-minute prelude either to infantry attack or to the placing of a demolition charge. Defenders were not just burned but asphyxiated, blinded by smoke, or simply terrified into surrender at the first bellowing burst.[7]

Goch, Germany, 21 February 1945: during the clearance of snipers from the factory area a Tommy identified as a Sgt J.Welch, from Gateshead, shows good street-fighting technique. Rather than raising himself to fire through the window, the NCO stays low and aims from a ragged hole in the wall below, where the outline of his No.4 rifle is at least partially disguised among the debris of masonry and furniture. At Goch, British flamethrowers and armour were successfully employed in support of the attack by 51st (Highland) Division.

The British made good use of flamethrower tanks and carriers as well as man-pack equipment, the vehicles having considerable advantages in terms of operator protection, increased fuel stowage and thus duration, and increased range – the Churchill 'Crocodile' flame tank had a maximum range of over 100 yards. By the end of the war the fruits of experience were summarized in the *Tactical Handling of Flame-Throwers* (1945). Their 'neutralizing' value on enemy firing positions was considered uniquely high: at the first hint of flamethrowers in the area the enemy would be pre-occupied by fear of becoming a target; if 'flamed', they were at least blinded by the smoke, and forced to abandon the position if it took fire, and a man who got a blob of burning fuel on him had no thought for anything else.

Limited fuel capacity was certainly a handicap, but British tactics sought to minimize its impact by fuel economy during an approach, and by using flame weapons in numbers, so that they could 'leapfrog' past each other as they were expended. The effects of an attack could be increased by hosing a target with unignited 'wet shots' before lighting it up with a subsequent burst of flame to produce a massive conflagration.

In towns and villages fortified buildings were treated exactly like pillboxes, and wooden or timber-framed structures naturally made exceptionally good targets for 'flaming'. During flame attacks both vehicle-mounted and man-pack units required fire support from tanks or infantry. The man-pack flamethrowers were 'best used in teams organised to provide close covering fire to enable the operator to work forward to his flaming position, and close escort to indicate targets and to lay smoke with smoke hand grenades'. Such teams were usually held as a reserve by an infantry battalion commander, and attached to a rifle company in action – well forward, so as to be ready for use according to a plan devised by the 'flame commander' under the direction of the senior infantry officer. To achieve sufficient 'mass', flame tanks were best

[7] See Elite 160, *World War II Infantry Assault Tactics*

used in a minimum of half-squadrons (half a dozen tanks), and carriers and man-packs in sections of at least three weapons. A reserve, or a second wave, was required for replacements or exploitation, and the 'broader the front and the greater the number of flamethrowers used the greater normally is the success of the operation, since the moral effect on the enemy increases out of all proportion to the increase in numbers used'.

CONCLUSIONS

In 1939 European and US armies had a common perception that street fighting was unpleasant, costly, and likely to be strategically unrewarding. The Germans had at least a theoretical lead in urban tactics, recognizing that if it became necessary then the task would require combined-arms groups similar to those used in attacks on fortifications. British concepts were generally more sketchy, though the use of buildings as strongpoints, and the employment of engineers in the preparation of defences, were familiar themes. A choreographed plan for street fighting was still being evolved in 1940, and the US forces were even less well prepared.

The shock of Germany's rapid victories in 1939–40 was a tactical wake-up call to the Allies, though as yet relatively little town-fighting had been seen. It was in fact the British Home Guard – today dismissed by the ignorant as a laughable 'Dad's Army' – that was at the forefront of developing new street-fighting techniques, being inspired by models drawn from the Spanish Civil War, and by the realization that their role might well be that of fighting sacrificial delaying actions.

Bremen, Germany, mid-April 1945: men of the 1st Bn South Lancashires from 3rd Inf Div show textbook technique during the clearance of factories in this riverport city, which took nine days' fighting to secure. They have climbed up to a roof before entering a building and clearing it from the top downwards. A junior NCO with a Sten SMG darts forward, followed by a Bren team – the LMG was useful for mounting high up to give covering fire.

It was only after the invasion of Russia that street battles became commonplace, and the breakdown of the sweeping German armoured thrusts into more traditional 'bite and hold' actions then turned street fighting into a staple of infantry combat. Some of the earliest Soviet attempts at defending towns were spectacularly incompetent, and ended abruptly with settlements being outflanked or seized by combined German infantry-engineer combat teams. The involvement of German (and local) political murder squads, and Soviet reluctance to evacuate places which their propaganda declared could not fall, turned many a town in the western USSR into a slaughterhouse. In 1942–43, when the Wehrmacht was increasingly exhausted at the end of extended supply lines, Hitler's obsession with territorial symbols landed them in set-piece urban battles such as Stalingrad; here the Red Army demonstrated just how much they had learned, ensuring that street battles would be viciously fought and often very evenly balanced.

Another photo taken during the fighting to clear Bremen, 17–26 April 1945, showing a Bren-gunner from a 52nd (Lowland) Div unit covering a rubble field between factory buildings. The surviving concrete structure to his right is a Luftschutz air raid sentry post.

The learning curve of the Western Allies, who had so far absorbed many of the new ideas only at a distance, shot up abruptly with the invasion of Italy. British, US, Canadian, New Zealand, Indian and Free Polish forces were all involved in actions that demonstrated not only the value of established street-clearing drills, but the vital need for the co-ordination of aircraft, artillery and armour with the infantry. One result was the landmark British manual *Fighting in Built Up Areas* (1943); another was the US *FM 31-50*, which drew heavily on German tactical models.

In the case of street fighting, as in many other tactical specifics, it is clear that the prime mechanism in the US Army's adoption of effective new methods was a convergence between the US and German doctrines. Passages were lifted unaltered from enemy manuals, and practical lessons learned from the enemy on the battlefield were disseminated – for example, through publications such as US First Army's *Battle Experiences* series, and the War Department *Information* bulletins and *Combat Lessons*. British improvements followed a similar pattern, but also built on models evolved in 1940–42, including Home Guard literature and *The Instructor's Handbook on Field Craft and Battle Drill*.

After the failed Ardennes offensive of December 1944 fuel shortages and the virtual extinction of an already depleted Luftwaffe drastically reduced German mobile operations. Under such circumstances fixed defences, and especially resistance zones based on towns and cities, became crucial. Allied ability to overcome such defence may have been based on artillery, airpower and armour, but its final success depended on a continued willingness to engage in street fighting. Inside the Reich, the imminent arrival of the Western Allies persuaded many communities that it was time to hang out the white flags; nevertheless, last-ditch defence was official policy, and the attempted surrender of even insignificant villages often brought Party reprisals. In the East, for obvious reasons, resistance was the rule.

Fighting in built-up areas remains a dirty business; and regular armies, even those with highly developed tactical urban warfare skills, still seek to avoid it, to the present day.

Victory: in Cleve, Germany, April 1945, a British Tommy – slung around with extra personal equipment that gives him the characteristic look of a badly wrapped parcel – is posed hooking a banner from a window in Herzog-Strasse. (IWM HU 63665)

SELECT BIBLIOGRAPHY

Altner, Helmut, *Berlin: Dance of Death* (Staplehurst, UK, 2002)
Ambrose, Stephen E., *Citizen Soldiers* (London, 2002)
Bastable, Jonathan, *Voices from Stalingrad* (Newton Abbott, UK, 2006)
Beevor, Anthony, *Stalingrad* (London, 1998)
Citino, Robert M., *The Path to Blitzkrieg: Doctrine and Training in the German Army* (Boulder, CO, 1999)
Cole, Hugh M., *The Battle of the Bulge* (Washington, DC, undated r/p)
Cuthbert, Capt S.J., *We Shall Fight in the Streets* (r/p Boulder, CO, 1985)
Chuikov, Vasili Ivanovich, *The Battle for Stalingrad* (New York, 1964)
Davies, Norman, *Rising 44: The Battle for Warsaw* (London, 2004)
Ellis, John, *Cassino: The Hollow Victory* (London, 1984)
MacDonald, Charles B., *Company Commander* (Washington, DC, 1947)
Mueller, Ralph, et al, *Report After Action: The Story of the 103rd Infantry Division* (Innsbruck, 1945)
Pallud, Jean-Paul, 'Budapest', in *After the Battle*, 40 (London, 1983)
Wigram, Maj Lionel, *Battle School 1941* (r/p Cambridge, UK, 2005)
Wartime manuals are specifically cited in the text.

PLATE COMMENTARIES

A: STREET-FIGHTERS
A1: British Home Guard sniper, 1942
This design for an urban camouflage smock and hood is taken directly from patterns and full instructions in *The Home Guard Fieldcraft Manual* (1942); the author, Maj John Langdon-Davies, intimates that identical costume was also used by regular troops at that date. The smock and hood were cut loosely from folded tabard-shapes of hessian, and stitched up to leave irregular flaps down the sides to help break up the outline. The suit has an oblong eye section left partially covered by uncut threads, rather than conspicuous round eyeholes; a slanted slit in the breast gives access to ammunition for the P14/P17 rifle, in the battledress pocket beneath. This home-painted camouflage pattern is No.3 of several illustrated designs; for urban warfare the author recommended hard-edged blocks of dark brown and brick-red on the natural hessian background.

A2: 'Lightning' gunner, Gurt Battalion, Polish Home Army; Warsaw, August 1944
This was one of the units that fought in defence of Warsaw city centre during the Rising. Like most, its 'uniform' was essentially improvised, using elements from civilian work clothing, civil services uniforms and captured German items, with a white-and-red brassard as the single unifying feature. The Gurt fighters mostly wore dark blue, often with a cap – this example is a German railwayman's, with added Polish eagle badge and national flash. About 700 examples of the Blyskawica or 'Lightning' SMG, designed by Waclaw Zawrotny and Seweryn Wielanier, were produced in small secret workshops from the end of 1943, and most were used in the Rising; its extensive use of screwed rather than welded components made dispersed production practical. Its design drew upon both the Sten and the MP 40; it weighed just over 3kg (6.6lb), took the common 9mm parabellum ammunition, and had an effective range of about 100 yards – perfectly adequate for close-range street battles. In the background, note the Home Army's *kotwica* or 'anchor' emblem; this incorporated the letters 'PW' (for *Polska Walczaca*, 'Fighting Poland'), the P sometimes rendered as a sabre hilt.

A3: Flamethrower operator, Queen's Own Rifles of Canada, 3rd Canadian Division; Normandy, June 1944
The D-Day landings saw the first combat use of the Mk II version of the British Flamethrower, Portable, No.2 – nicknamed the Lifebuoy because of the doughnut shape of its fuel tank. It shared the drawbacks of its foreign counterparts: it was heavy (64lb); the ignition of the fuel jet, initiated by a small electric battery, was ureliable; and the capacity of 4 Imp gals (18.6 litres) gave only about ten 2-second bursts, to a range of no more than 40 yards even with thickened fuel. Refilling the tank, and replacing the spherical central reservoir holding the pressurized nitrogen/carbon dioxide propellant mixture, took about 5 minutes; and the position of the fuel valve under the right side of the tank was awkward for the operator to reach.

This private, from one of the assault units of 3rd Canadian Div which landed on Juno Beach on 6 June, carries tools and small spares in a single basic pouch, a revolver for self-defence, and a slung respirator. Flamethrowers were provided to infantry units on request rather than being standard issue, so their effectiveness was further reduced by the shortage of properly qualified operators; however, they remained a terrifying addition to the Allied troops' street-fighting arsenal. (This figure is based on photographic reconstructions by Philippe Guérin et al in *Militaria* magazine No.251, June 2006.)

B: HOME GUARD 'DEFENDED LOCALITY'; Yarrow Bridge, Lancashire, UK, 1941
This is closely based on an original Home Guard defence plan now held by the Museum of Lancashire collections, for A4 Platoon, 12th (Leyland) Bn, East Lancashire Home Guard, whose mission was to help defend one of the vital Leyland Motor Works outside Chorley. This defended locality scheme was unique in its details, but typical of hundreds of others.

The key topographical features are Bolton Road and its main crossing at Yarrow Bridge, in the wooded Yarrow river valley south-east of the motor works; holding this bridge would make it difficult for any attacker to move quickly on the factory complex. Note that while about half the platoon are positioned forward to control the crossing and its approaches from trenches and weapon pits, the remainder are held back

In early 1945, two Red Army combat engineers with flamethrowers move through gardens behind a street of German houses. They are burdened by the 23.5kg (51lb) weight of the latest ROKS-3 flamethrower, with the small cylinder of compressed-air propellant mounted beside the large 10.4 litre fuel cylinder. Unseen here, the fuel pipe terminated in a projector tube made to resemble a rifle; this was a legacy of the ROKS-2, which had a box-shaped tank in a canvas backpack, and was supposed to be a surprise weapon. Both types had ten ignition cartridges in a drum at the muzzle, and it was claimed that the fuel load gave the ROKS-3 ten 5-second bursts; the range was only 15m with unthickened fuel. See commentary, Plate A3. (Private collection)

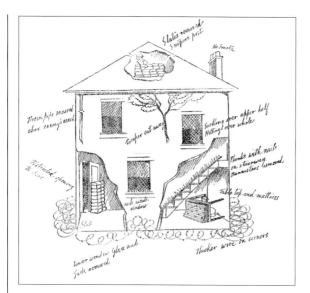

Various handwritten annotations on the illustration: "Static sandbag snipers post"; "No Smoke"; "Drain pipe removed above enemy reach"; "timber cut away"; "Sacking over upper half"; "Netting over whole"; "Planks with nails on stairway banisters removed"; "Table top and mattress"; "Restricted opening to door"; "nail coated window"; "Lower windows Glass and Lath removed"; "thicker wire on corners"

How to prepare a house for defence, from the British manual *The Instructors' Handbook on Fieldcraft and Battle Drill* (1942). The measures include the construction of a sandbagged sniper's post in the attic; attaching wire netting to prevent grenades being thrown through windows, and sacking curtains inside the upper half to create shadow and mask movement; pulling drainpipes and creepers off the walls to prevent them being used as handholds for climbing; covering the stairs with nail-studded planks, and breaking away the banisters; making a corner barricade of furniture and matresses under the stairs; jamming the door partly shut with sandbags (earth-filled chests of drawers were also recommended); and laying barbed wire around the exterior.

Projector; and finally, Ptes Hargreaves and Russell are listed as 'sanitary' personnel… Most importantly, L/Cpl King also leads a ten-man 'battle section' or reserve force held at Yarrow House to deploy against any emerging threat.

All the forward elements have pre-prepared alternate positions – **(B1, C1, D1 & E1)** – to which they can move if compromised or requiring a different field of fire. If Yarrow House becomes untenable or the platoon need to withdraw closer to the motor works, the tennis club at **A1** is the alternate HQ. From here the platoon can defend a fall-back position among the houses just outside the factory complex, as well as from Halliwell's Farm, which commands the route from the tunnel under the railway embankment.

(Inset 1) Schematic of Lt Hanson's half-platoon at Yarrow House: (from top) HQ element and runners; first aid element; battle section, plus Northover Projector – a smoothbore 2.5in barrel projecting anti-personnel or AT grenades by a black-powder charge; transport element; sanitary personnel.

(Inset 2) Spigot mortar or 'Blacker bombard' – here mounted on a pivot pin in a concrete block, but also issued with a cruciform low-level ground mounting. This fired a 20lb fin-stabilized AT warhead to an effective range of c.100 yards, or an anti-personnel round to c.500 yards. The weapon weighed 350lb and needed a crew of five or six to move it.

(Inset 3) US M1917 water-cooled MG; and rifleman in foxhole or slit trench with overhead camouflage. Home Guard manuals made much of the need for intelligent concealment, in both countryside and urban settings.

(Inset 4) Home Guard section manning slit trench. Average age was 30, produced by a mixture of pre-conscript teenagers keen to 'do their bit', and men of 40–55, many of whom had Great War experience. Instructors noted the need to re-educate such veterans that there was no 'front line' to be held to the last, and that they must think in terms of flexible, mobile, all-round defence.

as a reserve/strike force. Another crucial point is that while the scheme uses buildings intelligently, it does not include a slavish, last-ditch static defence of isolated houses which would be magnets for enemy fire. Structures and the spaces between them are used to mount a flexible defence, with a strike force held back to respond to any attack. Other platoons of A Coy would simultaneously control defended localities east of the railway embankment, and to the west of Carr Cottages; the last line of defence might have to be in the built-up areas of the factories and town centres, but the purpose of this scheme was to buy time.

It is interesting to note that the original LDV (later HG) battalions were planned as 1,500 strong, later rationalized to 1,000 men. Here we see that a single 'platoon' (one **red dot** = one man) numbers no fewer than 57 all ranks including 2 officers, 2 sergeants, 11 corporals and lance-corporals. In addition to small arms – P17 rifles, at least one Thompson SMG, grenades and improvised 'Molotov cocktails' – the platoon has a medium machine gun, a spigot mortar and a Northover grenade projector.

At **(RB)**, Lt Carrington covers a roadblock at the bridge with Sgts Edge and Scholes and Cpl Naylor. The rest of his half-platoon are dug in well out of sight: at **(C)** Cpl Marsden and five men at Yarrow Bridge trench, positioned in the woods to give views eastwards along the river to the road, and southwards to the weir in Mill Wood; and at **(B)** Cpl Hough and five men, controlling the secondary Hogg's Lane Bridge over Black Brook. The best support weapons, the MMG **(D)** and the spigot mortar **(E)**, are in prepared positions further back, with fields of fire down the Bolton Rd to the roadblock, or to face any flanking movement from the east or west. The distances to the bridge, the pub beyond it, Higher Red Bank, the LMS railway line, and other features have all been ranged in advance.

At **(A)**, Yarrow House, the platoon commander Lt Hanson has the HQ element – Cpl Prescott and five junior ranks, of whom the Simm brothers provide short-range communication with the forward areas by means of a bicycle and a motorbike. L/Cpl Fishwick leads a five-man first aid section, and two privates man the transport – presumably a civilian lorry. L/Cpl Lee and two privates man the Northover

C: RED ARMY 'STORM GROUP'; Stalingrad, autumn 1942

A 'storm group', drawn from the resources of a specific rifle battalion, has been tasked with taking a building in an industrial quarter of the city. The total attack force **(red dots)** is of weak company strength, bolstered with attached machine guns and other support assets, such as combat engineers with demolition charges, to a total of perhaps 100 men. The German defenders **(blue dots)** number less than a platoon – say about 20 men (here, any support from other buildings is only roughly indicated by random numbers of

Operation 'Market-Garden', September 1944: a British officer armed with a .38in Enfield revolver. The manual *Fighting in Built Up Areas* observed that 'The pistol in practised hands is a useful weapon for very close quarter fighting, as when searching a house. In unskilful hands the weapon is more likely to disconcert, if not actually endanger our own troops'. If this man is in a combat area then he is making a basic tactical error: he is too close to the window, and from outside the building he is likely to be framed in the middle of an obvious aperture.

blue dots). The preliminary phases of the attack are not shown, but were typically as follows:

First phase: During the previous 24 hours Soviet scouts and snipers worked their way forward through the cover of ruins and rubble, to ascertain the enemy numbers and positions, the possible avenues of approach, and fields of fire. During daylight hours one or two MGs and/or other heavy weapons were zeroed-in on fixed lines. Automatic fire directed at embrasures will hamper the eventual defence of the strongpoint against assault.

Second phase: During the night or under cover of smoke, the 'assault teams' creep forward towards the target under cover of rubble, over rooftops, or by avenues not swept by the defenders' fire. Soviet fire on fixed lines helps cover their approach. We show four assault teams **(A)**, totalling about 25–35 men, led forward to suitable jumping-off positions in the ruins by a small command element **(C)**. Together these comprise the first or 'assault wave' of the 'storm group'. They take cover as close as possible to the target – within grenade-throwing range, and to make it difficult for enemy artillery, mortars, aircraft or armour to target them without endangering their own men.

Third phase: This is the action illustrated. On the signal, the assault teams attack the strongpoint, hurling grenades and firing as they charge in to engage the remaining defenders at hand-to-hand range. The four teams assault simultaneously but independently, under continuing covering fire from the four nearby 'reinforcement teams' **(R)** and heavy weapons **(MG)**. As soon as the assault teams gain entry, the reinforcement teams rush forward in their turn, from different angles and using fire-and-movement if necessary. They bring LMGs, HMGs, AT rifles and demolition charges with them; after

providing support to the assault teams, once the building has been cleared they consolidate the new position, setting up the heavy weapons to meet any immediate counter-attack. They are accompanied by the command element.

Fourth phase: If the assault is unsuccessful, the commander feeds his two reserve platoons **(RSV)** into the fighting as a third wave. If it is successful, then he sends them forward to occupy the vacated positions of the reinforcement squads, or to create blocking groups or flanking positions to defend the captured building. Additional ammunition and stores are carried up to the new front line.

(Inset 1) A typical assault team, of six to eight men led by a junior NCO, were armed for heavy short-range firepower with SMGs, grenades and/or Molotov cocktails, knives and entrenching tools.

(Inset 2) The command element for the assault wave: typically, a junior officer with a signal pistol and flares, supported by two or three runners or a signaller with a field telephone. One of the party carries a small red flag, to mark the building as a signal that it has been secured.

(Inset 3) A typical reinforcement squad, of about eight men: here, a junior NCO with an SVT semi-automatic rifle, and two-man teams with a Maxim heavy MG on its wheeled carriage, a DP light MG and an AT rifle, supported by one or more riflemen/ammunition carriers or sappers.

(Inset 4) One of the two reserve platoons, about 20 strong. The 40-odd men would be led by an officer of company commander status; though mainly composed of riflemen, they might include a couple of snipers, a further HMG team and a couple of LMG teams.

D: BRITISH HOUSE-CLEARING DRILL, 1943–45

The drill explained in *Fighting in Built Up Areas*, the British 'bible' of urban warfare from 1943, was expected to be a 'guide and basis for training', to be modified depending upon the details of the building attacked.

First phase: The infantry section has worked its way into the garden of a detached house by fire-and-movement, and has broken down into two elements: the 'covering group' with the Bren team and three riflemen; and the 'clearing group' – the section commander **(C)**, a bomber **(B)**, first and second entry men **(E1 & E2)**, and a look-out **(L)**. The Bren and the rest of the covering group engage the house with fire, shooting at any targets in doors and windows and covering any entrances and exits that might allow the enemy defenders to move from house to house or take counter-action. Under cover of this fire the section commander and bomber push forward to a convenient position from which to cover and direct the entry men through the most promising entrance. The commander has identified a back door ajar close to a large window; he fires his SMG to break the window, and then puts a second burst through the door; from one side, the bomber then throws a grenade through whichever presents the best target. As soon as it explodes the section commander signals the entry men forward.

Second phase: The two entry men dash in, get their backs against walls, aiming at any internal doors and shooting as needed. The look-out crouches near the door or window in a position that enables him to see and shoot inside or outside the house (he does not stand silhouetted in the doorway). When the entry men are safely in position the look-out signals the section commander accordingly. The entry men throw a grenade into the next room to be cleared, preparing for movement.

Third phase: The section commander and bomber now also enter the house, passing the entry men and moving rapidly from point to point, shooting as needed, as they make for the stairs; the bomber acts as the commander's immediate assistant and escort. (If well-trained, they will shoot low, so as to catch any kneeling defender, rather than at the normal height of the body's centre of mass.) The look-out remains at his post.

The commander now has to make a split-second decision. It is always preferable to take advantage of the defenders' initial surprise, and distraction by the fire from the covering group, to clear a house from the top downwards. Ideally the section commander should lead the way up the stairs as soon as he reaches them, rather than risking driving the defenders upstairs ahead of him, but this may not be possible; the stairs may be blocked, or there may be downstairs rooms which it is hazardous to leave uncleared. If there is stubborn resistance then the covering party may even have to be called inside the house to add their firepower.

In this illustration we show clearance of the final downstairs room first. On reaching the stairs safely, the commander leads the bomber and first entry man up, leaving the second entry man at the bottom to provide cover in several directions. The look-out holds his position, to provide cover and prevent any enemy from breaking out. Meanwhile, outside, the covering party prepare to move up.

(Inset) Having reloaded if necessary, the three men work from room to room upstairs, using grenades and bursts of fire to neutralize any defenders. Doors would be shot up before a grenade was thrown in.

Fourth phase: The clearance group reassemble on the ground floor; the look-out continues to watch the back of the house until the covering party have adopted positions around it to prevent any reinforcement or retreat. (In more open ground the Bren team might directly support the approach of the clearing party, before moving to cover the street and likely exits.)

E: US HOUSE-CLEARING DRILL, 1944–45

This illustration is based partly on two dramatic sketches from the seminal US manual FM 31-50. One shows the recommended method of attacking a terraced (row) house by coming in through a wall from an adjoining house, and clearing it from the bottom upwards. Unable to force access through the attic space, the GIs have blown themselves a 'mousehole' through on the ground floor with a TNT demolition charge. The shock of this powerful explosion, followed by rapid fire, has killed the defender of the downstairs room. Once through, the GIs then fire blind up through the ceiling, in an attempt to neutralize anyone in the bedroom above. While this continues, part of the squad simultaneously engage and neutralize a defender at the head of the staircase. They then mount the stairs, and the squad leader opens fire at floor level through the bedroom door, hoping to catch any defenders in a crossfire; the Thompson SMG was not standard issue for rifle platoons, but an experienced NCO might easily acquire one for this sort of work, where its short-range firepower and the heavy .45cal round would be valuable. However, the German has not yet

been hit. He has made himself a rudimentary 'corner barricade' with a table and a mattress; and until the GIs can reach the door and get a couple of grenades through, the chances of the leading attacker are uncertain.

Once they subdue all resistance and reach the upstairs windows the GIs will be well placed to signal their progress to comrades on the ground outside, and to observe and snipe any enemy nearby. Finally, they will have to clear the loft space – again, it will be safer to spray bullets through the ceiling before trying to boost one of their number up through the hatch. The solutions to tactical problems taught by FM 31-50 were tried, tested and sensible; however, the rate of attrition in this sort of room-to-room fighting could be terribly high, by its very nature.

Clearing a row of terraced houses from above or below: illustrations from a British manual, Col G.A. Wade's *House to House Fighting* (c.1940). Terraced rows offered some distinct advantages over detached structures (see Plate D). In Plate 11 the attackers enter the ground floor of the right-hand house and climb into the attic ('cock-loft'); in the 1940s these attic spaces were often undivided, so they can pass through into that of the adjoining house, then work their way downwards. In Plate 12 they 'mousehole' in from an adjoining cellar, then work their way upwards.

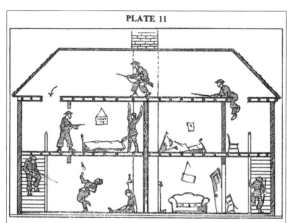

PLATE 11

ATTACK THROUGH COCK-LOFT

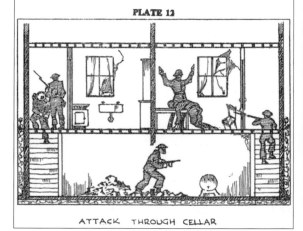

PLATE 12

ATTACK THROUGH CELLAR

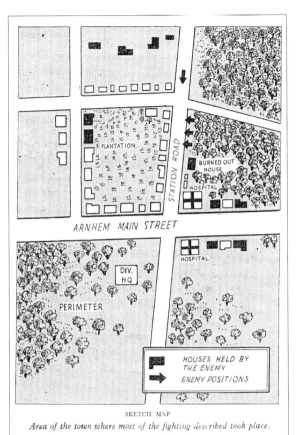

ARNHEM MAIN STREET

PLANTATION

STATION ROAD

BURNED OUT
HOUSE

HOSPITAL

HOSPITAL

DIV.
HQ

PERIMETER

HOUSES HELD BY
THE ENEMY

ENEMY POSITIONS

SKETCH MAP

Area of the town where most of the fighting described took place.

Plan from *Diary of a Glider Pilot* (1945), showing the spread-out villas of the Osterbeek suburb of Arnhem, and how the Germans succeeded in penetrating individual houses (black) so that eventually neighbouring buildings were held by men of the opposing sides. Middle-class suburbs with detached houses and large gardens required a mixture of true 'street fighting' and traditional fieldcraft – see Plate D.

F: *BARYKADY* FIGHTING; Warsaw, August 1944

A reconstruction of a typical few streets in Warsaw city centre, as defended by the Gurt Bn of the Polish Home Army **(blue dots)**. Their German opponents, probing from north to south, are an assault gun unit and armoured engineers; the Germans have learned to keep the bulk of their infantry back under cover **(red dots)**, and are waiting for the armour and engineers to breach the barricades before they advance through the buildings under covering fire.

At top, a StuG III armoured assault gun has turned the corner. Its way is being prepared by two engineers **(GE)** of a Panzerpionier Kompanie (Goliath), sheltering behind a pile of rubble and controlling by wire two of the small 'Goliath' remote-control, tracked, armoured explosive-carriers *(leichte Ladungsträger SdKfz 303)* with 150kg demolition charges **(G)**. The Poles have erected a so-called 'Little David' **(LD)** 10 or 20 yards short of the main barricade to prevent the Goliaths reaching it; this system, devised by university professors, was a line of paving slabs set upright in the ground.

(Inset 1) Polish sniper in attic, with loophole made by removing a few bricks from the front wall; alternate positions would give him fields of fire in several directions, and the chance to displace if he is spotted. Another sniper might be under cover of a chimney stack on the roof further down the same building, where he could give some support to the first.

(Insets 2 & 3) A group of suicidally brave young lads are placed closer to the barricades, to attack any Goliaths or AFVs that look as if they will reach them. Some, in an upper room, have Molotov cocktails to drop onto the vulnerable top armour; in the sidestreet, others have a single precious captured *Panzerfaust*, a pair of wirecutters to sever the control wires of the Goliath, a pistol and more improvised grenades.

The main barricade **(B)** is a substantial wall of lifted paving slabs, but its solidity is disguised by a front layer of lighter materials such as furniture. In fact the Poles did not try to hold the actual barricades, but kept under cover to the flanks, where direct fire was unlikely to do them much damage.

(Inset 4) A small group of Gurt Bn soldiers wait around a corner; they will either fight from the sidestreet, flanking the Germans if they cross the barricade, or will disappear into pre-prepared positions within buildings. Apart from the ubiquitous armbands in national colours they wear motley clothing – mostly dark blue in this unit, with some old Polish Army items, and some captured from the Germans. They are lightly armed with Mauser rifles, pistols and one or two SMGs; one has a slung haversack of *'filipinkis'* – locally made grenades, some of which used air-dropped Allied plastic explosives.

At bottom right **(and inset 5)**, women are clustered at an open manhole, using an improvised derrick to lower ammunition and other stores to men and women in the sewers below, who will carry them forward to fighting positions.

At bottom left **(and inset 6)**, a girl messenger aged no more than 14 is running along a communication trench to the concealed entrance of a command bunker. She perhaps carries a request from the commander at the barricade to the company commander for one of the few carefully hoarded PIATs and a machine gun to be brought up, to face what is obviously going to be a major assault (naturally, the company has not put everything 'in the shop window' straight away). Any reinforcements will be employed in positions back from the barricade, ambushing any enemy who force their way through.

G: US RIFLE PLATOON DEFENCE SCHEME; NW Europe, winter 1944

This illustration is based on the ideal given in FM 31-50, *Attack on a Fortified Position and Combat in Towns* (January 1944). This degree of area protection, as solid as a miniature fortress, was only possible if the troops had the time and materials to perfect it; in many circumstances only parts of the plan would be practicable.

The diagram shows **(blue dots)** only those men who were awake and on duty at any given moment. These 15-odd GIs constitute one 'relief'; the other relief is resting or otherwise employed, but will reinforce the defenders in the event of an attack. It was also desirable, particularly at night, to place sentries outside buildings (though not in obvious positions), the better to listen for and investigate movements and to raise the alarm.

Figure 29. Corner barricade.

An illustration from the manual FM 31-50 depicting the so-called 'corner barricade' – see Plate E. Knowing that a grenade was likely to be thrown into any occupied room first, German defenders sometimes erected an inner barricade using furniture and mattresses. From behind this they could hope to survive the explosion of the first grenade, and then shoot whoever followed it through the door. The recommended US antidote was to follow the first grenade with a second, lobbed into any corner that was suspiciously cluttered with furniture.

Each rifle squad was assigned a defined area of responsibility, and the suitability of every building was examined. Weak or flammable structures might be destroyed in advance, and fences, hedges, etc removed so as to improve fields of fire and to deny the enemy cover. Individual men and crew-served weapons were provided with alternate positions; and here, the paths leading into the central defended block have been obstructed with barbed wire.

The squad leaders were responsible for dividing their squads into two reliefs. They checked individual rifle positions – **(R)** – and fields of fire, supervised camouflage of loopholes and ensured that weapon muzzles were not visible beyond cover. The best loopholes were in unexpected places – under eaves or through holes in roofs, in deep shadows or behind vegetation. Best practice was to move from one loophole to another frequently; making dummy loopholes, and blocking some with sandbags when not in use, was also valuable. In dry weather ground was damped down around firing points – both real and dummy – to prevent tell-tale dust being kicked up.

In this scenario the enemy are expected to advance from the north, but the streets have been blocked to allow an all-round defence. At each corner, a defensive 'sandwich' has been created across the streets giving access to the central square, with barbed wire enclosing a line of anti-tank obstacles and a belt of anti-tank and anti-personnel mines. These obstacle zones are covered by men with anti-tank rifle grenades or bazookas **(GR/B)**. Enemy infantry or engineers will have to brave barbed wire and anti-personnel mines to force a passage for armour, and if the AFVs advance first, they will run into AT obstacles and mines while under fire from AT weapons.

This rifle platoon has been reinforced with an AT gun attached from the battalion's AT platoon; this, and a 60mm mortar from the rifle company's weapons platoon, have been placed in the central garden area at the heart of the defence. Each corner of the central block has not only an individual

rifleman but also a pre-prepared gun position for the AT gun **(R+GP)**, into which it can be manhandled at need.

(Inset 1) Rifleman with M7 launcher for M9A1 AT grenades; by this date two or three launchers were issued to each rifle squad. When using windows rather than concealed loopholes as firing points, it was vital for men to keep well back inside the room.

(Inset 2) Squad NCO checking the position of a 'bazooka-man' with a 2.36in rocket launcher; each rifle company had three as standard issue, but extras could be attached from other battalion elements. Although keeping watch from indoors this bazooka-man will have to leave the enclosed room before firing, to avoid the consequences of over-pressure from the backblast.

(Inset 3) .30cal 'light' machine guns, attached from the company weapons platoon, would be provided with alternate firing positions; for close defence they were usually placed close to ground level, while for longer-range use they were emplaced high, sometimes on roofs. Here an M1919A6 is carried down into a basement, to be set up inside a ground-level vent for close defence.

(Inset 4) An M1 57mm AT gun; by this date high explosive ammunition was also available, increasing its value for urban fighting. Weighing well over a ton, this weapon needed plenty of hands to drag it around alternate positions once its towing vehicle had withdrawn; the less powerful 37mm weighed less than half as much and was genuinely man-handleable.

(Inset 5) A rifleman is posted in one of the positions being prepared in the corners of the central block for the AT gun.

H: 'DER ORTSKAMPF': German attack on Soviet-held village, 1944–45

This is closely based on a scheme shown in *Unteroffizier und Mann*, a pamphlet produced jointly by the Nazi Youth Leadership organization and the General Staff to encourage youngsters to join the forces as early as possible. The details have been elaborated from Reibert, *Der Dienst Unterricht im*

French FFI (Forces of the Interior) irregulars photographed on the streets of Paris during the immediate pre-liberation phase in August 1944. There was serious street fighting by the Resistance in parts of the city, and some 1,500 Parisians died between 19 and 24 August; nevertheless, one cannot help wondering if the girl with the MP40 has not given as much thought to her appearance as to her task. (IWM AP 35764)

Heere, and the British manual *Tactics of the German Army: Attack and Pursuit* (July 1944).

A small East German or Polish village of mainly timber structures, in a clearing in woodland, is held by two platoons from a Red Army rifle company (**red dots**), reinforced with three Maxim heavy machine guns, and numbering about 50 men in all. They have not held the houses for long, and in frozen conditions have not developed many obstacles or fieldworks; however, they have laid a hasty minefield to protect two of the entrances into the village; constructed a bunker for one of the HMGs; and dug or blasted a couple of section trenches and some foxholes on the perimeters. The other two HMGs are emplaced in cover, flanking the front of the houses, some of which have been prepared internally for defence.[8]

The German attack plan is for a reinforced company (**blue dots** – fewer here than the actual number of men). One of the three companies from a 1944-type infantry battalion has roughly 100 men in three platoons; it has an attached HMG section and mortar section from the battalion heavy weapons company (two MG34s or 42s on sustained-fire mounts, and two 81mm mortars); an attached combat engineer platoon, including two flamethrower teams; and an infantry gun platoon of two 15cm guns from the regimental howitzer company – i.e. a further 100-odd men from the support and specialist elements.

H1: First and second phases

Before dawn the German commander sends a section-sized patrol (**P**), with scouts to the fore, towards the left flank of the village; they take advantage of uneven ground and vegetation to get as close as possible unseen. At the same time the commander establishes his own command and observation post near the edge of the trees. The reconnaissance soon has the desired effect of causing the Soviet MGs to open fire; before he hastily withdraws the patrol leader also manages to observe what he believes is evidence of a minefield on the left flank.

Having identified the locations of several Soviet weapons positions the German commander engages them with his mortars and HMGs from the woods, while the infantry guns begin to fire over the village, so cutting it off from support from the rear.

H2: Third and fourth phases

Taking advantage of this fire, the bulk of the German infantry begin an enveloping movement through the woods around the right flank of the village.

Some of the buildings now begin to burn. One of the infantry platoons, supported by its own section LMGs, attacks and neutralizes the Soviet right-flank HMG position; a second presses on to envelop the right rear of the village. On the left flank, one of the mortars displaces forwards under cover, and both engage the other two Soviet HMGs. When these have been neutralized, the mortars and infantry guns switch to firing smoke rounds to cover the infantry attack; the German HMGs, now masked by the frontal advance of the third infantry platoon, also displace forward to the flanks to support the assault. The engineers deploy their flamethrowers (**Fw**) against stubborn bunkers or fortified houses; more of these start to burn, driving out their defenders.

In the fourth phase the Soviets are under assault from several directions, and the fighting has closed to SMG and grenade range. Any attempted counter-attacks to the flanks are met by the German MGs. Realizing that they are close to being encircled, the Soviets attempt to retreat; some run into German positions established in the woods to the rear, while others escape to the left rear. Finally, the German force will complete the operation by burning down the remaining houses rather than trying to clear them individually.

(**Inset 1**) German infantrymen in the assault, the section led by its MG34 LMG gunner; although partly replaced with the MG42 by this date the earlier weapon was still in use. By the last six months of the war some sections had two LMGs, which would be placed on each flank of the assault line. A minority of the platoon would also have received the Sturmgewehr 43/44 variable-fire assault rifle.

(**Inset 2**) German 15cm sIG 33 heavy infantry gun.

[8] See Fortress 62, *Soviet Field Fortifications 1941–45*

INDEX